E-BANKING AND
BUSINESS MODELS

Lopamudra Ghosh
Dr. Ganesh Sambhaji Lande
Dr. P. Rengarajan
Dr. K. Bhavana Raj
Dr. Anil Tiwari

red'shine
Publication
INDIA

E-BANKING AND BUSINESS MODELS

by: Lopamudra Ghosh, Dr. Ganesh Sambhaji Lande, Dr. P. Rengarajan, Dr. K. Bhavana Raj, Dr. Anil Tiwari

■

RED'SHINE PUBLICATION PVT. LTD.

Headquarters (India): 88-90 REDMAC, Navamuvada,
Lunawada, India-389 230
Contact: +91 76988 26988
Registration no. GJ31D0000034

In Association with,

RED'MAC INTERNATIONAL PRESS & MEDIA. INC

India | Sweden | UK

■

ISBN: 978-93-93239-47-1
ISBN-10: 9-39-323947-9
DIP: 18.10.9393239479
DOI: 10.25215/9393239479
Price: ₹ 400
December, 2021 (First Edition)

■

www.redshine.co.in | info@redshine.in
Printed in India | Title ID: 9389476232

E-BANKING AND
BUSINESS MODELS

CONTENTS

MODULE-1

INTRODUCTION TO PRESENT DAY BANKING SYSTEM

The banking division is act as a key position in the economic expansion of any nation. The expansion of the bank division relies on the services it provides in the direction of customer in a variety of sectors. In India the increasing state of bank services is important for the original economic development. Now, India has a vast banking system with different banking sections banking – by state, foreign banks, private equity banks, regional banks and co-operative banks by RBI India as a main structure chief.

Now the bank division serves as the backbone of the Indian financial system, which acts as catalyst for growth and development. Since 1991 a variety of development have been identified in the banking sector. It also highlights the range of changes that have been made to get better their services to thc satisfaction of customer.

India has a great population with diverse culture, and a wide diversity of income, marked between the nations. A lot of level of illiteracy of a huge fraction of the people but, at the similar, the nation has great talent for management skills and technological advancement. About 30 to 35 percent of the people lives in large cities and towns and some have spread too little city and rural areas. The nation financial plan formation includes social and capitalist elements that are highly biased for community division savings. India has followed the way of increase leading to exports instead of "enlargement leading to exports" to other Asian economies, with an importance on foreign exchange assurance. These factors are reflecting in the arrangement, mass, variety of the nation banking and financial division.

The bank structure is required to attain the economic policy objectives set out in the five-year development plans, mainly with regard to equitable distribution of income, fair regional financial enlargement, and the decrease of corporate commercial and industrial violence. For the banking business to function as a position policy tool, it was incorporated under a variety of nationalization programs at different stages (1955, 1969, and 1980). As a result, banks are isolated on a global scale (with a few Indian banks located overseas in international financial institutions) due to concerns over important domestic matters, especially local office enlargement.

In adding, the division is tasked with providing hold up for other sectors of the economy like agriculture sector, small scale industries, and banking services in residential marketable areas (i.e., metro, city, and a partial number of small towns Institutions). The division of the global banking system is due to the strict regulation of branch licenses for existing foreign banks already in use in the nation and the entry limits in front of new distant banks. A condition of reconciliation is necessary for the bank in India to undo a workplace overseas. These factors have left the Indian banking part weak and strong. A major confront opposite Indian banks, under the present patent framework, how they can attain the optimal efficiency of modern financial interventions.

NEW TRENDS IN BANKING

In addition, the sector is tasked with as long as hold up to other financial sector such as agriculture, exports, and banking services to residential marketable areas (i.e., metro, city, and Institutions).

Fragmentation of the global banking system is owed to the firm regulation of existing foreign bank branch licenses and the restrictions on access to new distant banks. A condition of reconciliation is necessary for any bank in India to release a workplace out of the country. These factors have left the Indian banking sector weak and powerful. The biggest confront in front of Indian banks, below the current patent framework, is how they can achieve the effectiveness of current financial interventions. Taking place the other, it has been easier for state-owned banks to repay loans, agreed the increase in non-performing assets (NPAs), as state rights has condensed profit that will face by the private banks.

There have been new inventions and variations in the function of large marketable banks.

A number of occupied in the area of customer debt, credit cards, merchant banks, online banking and telephone, rental, joint ventures etc. A few banks have established subsidiary banks, leasing and joint ventures and many more are already in place.

GROWTH IN BANK DIVISION

Internet

The Internet is a system of computer in which connection can be transmitted or established universal. The Data can send and established in any division of the globe. In an instant, the Internet site do lot of work. It include: The network serve as an electronic mail system. It can contact a distant website, which can be a foreign newspaper. Customers can change their ideas online and can communicate with anyone connected to the internet. On the Internet, one can swap mail, information / drawings or recorded music.

The Internet is a rapid -growing and important network for community works, Educational institution, investigate association etc.

Automated Teller Machine (ATM)

An ATM is an electronic device used by a customer to deposit money, withdraw money. ATMs are the fastest way to improve customer service. The location of ATM is accessible to the customer 24 hours of a day. An ATM card is given to a customer customer who is a plastic card, with name written on it. In the card has a magnetic code and is read by the machine. All cardholder is given the ID number called PIN. When the customer uses the card, he has to insert the card in the machine. Once the card is identified by the machine, the customer put their ID number.

Then receiving customer confirmation, the ATM follows the customer to go through the amount to be issued by him. After considering the purchase and getting enough balance in his account, the ATM withdrawal facility provides him with the necessary cash. When the mission is completed, the ATM issues the customer card.

Cash Dispensers

Withdrawals are an important service provided by bank branches. Cash payment by cash or cash producer is another time saver. The operation of the machine is less expensive than the real operation and this machine quicker than that of an ATM. The customer is given a plastic card which is magnetically bounced. After official filling, the machine allows the machine to deal at the requisite cost.

Electronic Clearing Service

In year 1994, the RBI appointed a committee to review the banking system. The commission suggested in its statement that electronic payments should be made available to all government agencies / organizations by making a refundable payment such as bonus, interest, repayment, salary, pension or commission. The Details of the Electronic Clearing Service is provided in advance of the pre-authorized deductions to pay arrears, insurance premiums and rental installments with finance companies. The RBI has been an important step in launching these programs.

Bank net

The central bank is India's primary countrywide stage group, recognized in FEB , 1991. The message system was recognized by the RBI on the foundation of the advice of a group chosen by of chief executive T.N.A. Lyre. The bank balance is divided into two categories: net-I bank and net II bank

Chip Card

The bank customer is given a particular kind of credit card with the customer name, code. The quantity of the customer financial credit debt is record on a card by magnetic fields. The computer can check the magnetic field. When a customer uses the card, the sum of credit written on the card start to reduce. Subsequent to using the number of times, in one stage, the balance becomes a little on the card. At that point, the card is useless. The customer have to put the cash into his or her account in arrange to use again the card. And the sum of credit is printed on the card by magnetic resources.

Phone Banking

Customers can call the bank's default phone number and by dialing his or her ID number you will be able to access the designated bank computer. The software on the computer asks him to dial the code for the service code he wants and to respond properly. By using Automatic voice recorder (AVR) with easy queries and functions and phone terminal handled with complex questions, the customer can perform all cashless banking transactions: Anywhere, Anytime.

Tele-banking

Tele banking is one of the most advanced, allowing customers to bank at any time of day or night. Tele banking uses a voice processing system that is installed on bank computers. Customers can phone their bank at any time to inquire about their account balance or other transaction history. Bank computers are connected to a telephone connector via a modem in this configuration. The software includes a voice processing facility. This software recognises the caller's voice and provides the appropriate response. A telephone operator is also used by some banks, although only for specific temporary services. This is a telephone answering service that has evolved into Tele-banking. As the length of questions at ATMs grows longer, telephone banking is becoming increasingly popular.

Internet Banking

Online banking helps customer to perform banking services from side to side an online banking website. It is a system for accessing accounts and generalization for online banking products and services as sitting in the office or at home. This is called virtual banking. According to banking tradition, a person should come to the branch, withdraw cash or make a check or ask for a report of statement, etc. At present everybody can access all types of activities on their computer via the bank website. Every one such dealing is encrypted; uses security structures with many complex layers, including fire walls and filters. One can be sure that their work is secure and confidential.

Bio- metric authentication

For the purpose of safety bio-metric validation plays a major role. Several day organizations now use bio-metric validation.

CORE BANK SYSTEM

Core banking system is required in daily routine of bank. It is an essential fraction of bank expertise aimed at assisting their customers and with advanced services.

Core is short for "Centralized Online Real-time Exchange." since the given name suggest, it is a middle organization or network formed by a bank. This permits bank customer to right of entry and run essential resources at any bank branch to which they have an account. Thus, the central bank software permits banks to build a central data center.

Usually, Core Banking is thoroughly linked with the profitable banking sector. So, banks are at the present committed to expanding the range of the banking system outside of bank provisions. The basic banking system use in order to message for

Technology as a stage for it's a variety of request to facilitate banking processes and procedures.

Features of Core Banking Systems

Core banking system is an application by banks to give core banking solutions to customer. It chains banks in performing and recording the essential function of banks. Most of this system is designed to meet the wants and specifications of banks. Therefore, each system is different. a number of most excellent example of Indian banking software application are Infosys Finacle, Oracle Financial Services Software for Oracle Corporation.

Some of the key features of core banking systems are:

- giving out and replacement money deposits and cash removal
- cunning credit interest
- dispensation loans
- scheming and organization interest rate
- maintain customer association

Advantages of Core Banking Services

Banking and financial institutions have benefited hugely the acceptance of core banking systems. At the similar instance, customer evenly enjoys technology services. In banks, banking has become an integral part of their daily operations and provides great support. Eliminate the need for deadly and unnecessary tasks. Evaluating, managing and improving data has become much easier with the introduction of an automated banking system. At the same time, it has augmented staff competence and output. Power and skill put to good use.

Additionally, it permits employees to make stronger their connection with the customer. Ultimately, it enables the bank to uphold a strong customer support.

For customer, system has introduced the idea of banking anytime. Compared to conventional banking systems, major banking services are much simpler and basic. Customers do not have to visit their bank branch each occasion they require to carry out basic banking services. They now have more accessible stations, such as mobile banking, internet banking, and ATMs. New information quickly and in real time. Lastly, it has a variety of offer banking products that are able to be found anywhere. In simple terms, basic banking is easy, fast, and expensive; and makes monitor easier.

It is clear that central banking system has approach an extended way. The introduction of new technologies such as block chain, Artificial Intelligence and extra, it is sure that the banking sector will experience one more kind of transformation. It's now a substance of time, basic banking determination be the only way to bank. At the time of the digital launch, the RBI aimed to implement 100% of India's central banking

INTERNET BANKING:

Online banking helps the customer to make financial dealings online. Online banking is recognized as online banking or web banking. Online banking includes deposits, transfers, and online payments. Almost all banking institutions have some form of online banking, which is accessible on both pc and mobile applications. With online banking, consumers do not have to visit a bank branch to cover the majority of their essential bank actions. All of this they can do as they please, wherever they wish, i.e. at home, at work, or on the way to our work. To access the, customer require to list their online banking service. To register, they require making a password. Once that is complete, they can occupy the app to manage all their banks. Online banking services vary from institution to institution. Many banks typically give essential services such as money transfers and housing payments. A number of banks permit customer to unlock new accounts and relate for a credit card online.

Features of Internet Banking

The customer use the services to ways transactional and non-transactional tasks which includes

- The customer can sight description statement.
- It is 24 x 7 services
- The customer can verify the history of the transactions. Like Bank, statements, various types of forms, applications can be downloaded.
- The customer can move funds, pay any kind of bill, recharge mobiles, DTH.
- The customer can purchase and put up for sale on e-commerce platforms.
- The customer can spend and ways trade the customer can book, transport, travel packages, and medical parcels.

Advantages of Online Banking

Comfort is a main increase of online banking:

Basic banking services like as paying bills and transfers among accounts can be with no trouble done 24 hours a day, seven days a week, where the customer needs. Online banking is quick and well-organized: Funds can be moved among accounts approximately immediately, particularly if two financial records are kept in the similar facility. Buyers can unlock and shut the Application Number for a variety of online accounts, from set deposits to rising deposit financial records that usually present high interest rates. Consumers can also check their financial minutes frequently: By permitting those to keep their accounts secure. Overnight right of entry to banking in order provides early detection of fake action, thus serving as a protection next to monetary overcome or loss.

Online Bill Payment:

Single of the huge reimbursement of online banking is online billing payments. Having write check or fill out forms to pay off debts, once you have put up your online bank accounts, all that is wanted is a easy tick or click, as you can usually pay the bills automatically. By online billing, it is simple to direct your accounts from a single mid font and path expenditure coming in or out of your account.

Mobile Banking

Mobile Banking (M-Banking) is a state-of-the-art banking service that provides banking services via a mobile communication device such as a mobile phone or Personal Digital Assistant (PDA). That is, not put in one place.

The significance of Mobile Banking

Mobile banking allows customers to access financial services from anywhere. Businesses and business owners can keep track of time by using mobile apps to make payments or collect payments directly from customer on their phone numbers. It is the most popular among small and medium-sized businesses (SMEs), who are distinct in their own manner.

Banks can reduce service costs while keeping consumer acceptance by utilizing mobile technologies. This means that any bank customer can use his app to request a service, such as establishing an account, or arrange debit orders or other payments, allowing for a wide range of activities and, ultimately, enhancing business growth.

LICENSING OF BANKS

Licensing refers to the process of obtaining approval from a higher authority. Here the authorization of banking companies refers to the procedure of receiving consent from the Reserve bank of India to set up banking companies in India below the banking regulation Act 1949.

Licensing

Licenses are usually issued by the national banking regulator to applicant companies that meet their banking requirements. Requirements may include requirements for a very small amount of money, a small number of directors, the residence of shareholders, the distribution of shares, the disclosure of beneficial shareholders, among other matters. These properties may vary from place to place, and they may vary according to the type of license required. Some areas, sometimes called tax havens, have a reputation for being negligent or have poor standards for issuing bank licenses, licensing, for example, shell companies, or companies with designated directors, or unknown shareholders, etc.

Licensing may involve a lengthy, complex, and elaborate process, banking license There are many areas where banks can contribute. A standard bank license permits the bank to connect in all banking activities, such as retail banking, merchant profits, financial management, asset organization and trade. The applicant may apply for a limited bank license, such as an overseas bank license.

FINANCIAL INCLUSION

Financial inclusion is a kind of bank and fiscal services that persons can use. Its goal to engage everyone of the community by giving them with the main monetary facilities in respect of the profits or investments. It focuses on long-term financial solutions for the underprivileged.

DEFINITION:

FINANCIAL INCLUSION

is a plan to make sure right of entry to suitable monetary products and services necessary by all section of the general public and weak groups such as weak categories especially at affordable and transparent costs by normal institutional players. .

Investment will enable banks to provide loans to weak groups such as the weak groups and the low-income group at rational cost. It will also help banks to provide financial products in such areas and be able to know the implication of saving and invest.

Financial investment can help ease scarcity in India by investing in opportunities connected to monetary services available in India. Keywords: Inclusive growth, equity, financial opportunities, financial management, investment programs, excellence of life, poverty reduction.

OBJECTIVES OF FINANCIAL INCLUSION:

Investment can benefit society and the economy. Investment has the possible to create optimistic externalities: it leads to enlarged savings, investment and, consequently, stimulates growth processes.

It also provides a stage to focus on saving money, especially among low-income earners who have been living under financial pressure, especially due to the lack of savings, which puts them at risk.

The availability of bank services and products is intended to offer an important instrument to focus on the use of savings. It also creates lawful forms for non-bank loans that rely on unauthorized credit channels such as family, friends and moneylenders.

Timely, secure and transparent access to credit at legitimate banking stations will permit for a spirit of abundance to increase productivity and prosperity in rural areas. It will open the doors to legitimate remittance services for low-income and non-bankers, who are now forced to use all forms of informal and expensive forms of payment. Investment is now seen as a solution to the gaps and rewards for the distribution of government benefits and subsidies through direct transfer of benefits to beneficiaries' bank accounts instead of sponsoring products and making cash expenditure.

So, in general, Investment has the potential to bring masses of unregistered people into the formal banking system, to plan their savings, to make stronger the interests of their business by making debt available and thus contributing to the economy.

NEW REFORMS IN BANKING SECTOR

The banking sector removes long-term financial pressures and creates a well-organized, creative and gainful financial sector that permits for a systematic price adjustment process to improve efficient distribution of resources.

Private and international banks have also begun work to accelerate the technological transformation of the banking sector. Such as internet banking, Instant Payment Service), RTGS (Real Time Gross Settlement), have given customers access to banking services anywhere.

The government recently announced new banking reforms, including the establishment of a Development Finance Institution (DFI) infrastructure, the creation of an Unsatisfactory Bank to deal with the problem of malfunctioning assets (NPAs), and the privatization of state-owned banks (government banks). PSB) to reduce its stack.

It has moved from a mobile banking system, which combines customer access and opposite connections to digital banking, including branch banking complete likely by the new era, offline technology.

•

MODULE-2

INTRODUCTION OF CORE BANKING IN INDIA

Computer banking in India was about the 1980's. Primary effort was complete in 1981 and continued to be long-drawn-out in 1984. Indian banks are board on a program at the branch stage which is done with the help of MS-DOS base computers.

In 1988, RBI's Deputy Governor Dr. C Rangrajan put into practice the basic banking idea with the help of the place the base for services such as telebanking, off-site ATMs, customer storage space. In the 1990s there was a major change in the banks when private and foreign bank banks reached the Indian bank division. Fresh age group banks have shaped a competition for conventional bank kind.

These compulsory traditional banks to take on new banking systems. Progress has continued as a result of such things as global trade, liberation and the crackdown on TRAI (Telecom Regulatory Authority of India). All of helps the Indian administration and its regulator to carry technology at a inferior price. At the present, the bulk banks are on the trail to change.

The banking industry has benefited greatly from ever-changing technologies. The crash of core banking solutions has misrepresented the method money is managed and the way banks operate. The completion of the banking system is a milestone in the Indian banking sector. Continuing development suggests bright prospect. Basic bank is just the start, the forecaster's offer to India's paperless and branchless banking scheme.

DEFINITION

Core banking is often described a trade run by a bank organization by means of its own sales customer or little businesses. A lot of banks treat sell customer as their main bank customer and have a divide business line up for managing small businesses. A better business is run through the institutional bank part of the institute. The primary bank is basically deposit and lend.

Nowadays, many banks are using central bank application to hold up their operation where 'CORE' stands for "Centralized Online Real-time Environment". This earnings that every one bank twigs have right to use to applications in central data centers. It revenue that deposits are displayed right away on bank servers and the customer can withdraw cash deposited in any of the bank branches worldwide. This application at the present have the capacity to deal with the customer wants of companies that provide a wide-ranging bank solution. Typical banking activities will comprise deposit accounts, mortgages and expenditure. Banks make these facilities accessible at most stations such as ATMs, online banking and branches.

Usually, Core Banking is intimately linked by means of the profitable banking division of the profitable banking system. Though, owing to the increase in the figure of business customer, banks have realized that simple banking facilities can carry business banking solution.

So, banks are at the present devoted to expanding the range of the banking system outside of bank stores. a number of the fundamental banking solutions comprise deposit financial records, loans, expenditure and additional. By means of the assist of banking software, these are facilities complete obtainable to bank customers from side to side ATMs, online banking, mobile banking.

CHARACTERISTICS OF CORE BANKING

A core banking classification is a programme or piece of software that banks use to provide core banking services to their customers.

It enlists banks to perform and reproduce the functions that banks are required to perform. The majority of these systems are tailored to satisfy the needs and conditions of financial institutions.

As a result, each method is unique. Infosys Finacle, Oracle Financial Services Software for Oracle Corporation, and others are some of the best examples of Indian banking software.

1. Organizational features for customer associations, as well as a 360-degree customer view.
2. The ability to develop new items and attract new customers.
3. Banking analytics, including risk analysis, prosperity analysis, and resource reserve sharing and security organisation requirements.
4. Finance in the banking industry, as well as general ledger and reporting.
5. Banking channels, such as teller machines, side counter applications, mobile banking, and online banking.
6. The most effective workflow technique.
7. A comfortable running surface

OBJECTIVES OF CORE BANKING SYSTEM

The main reason of adopt key banking technologies is to get better customer experience. It ensures customer usability and banking "anytime and anywhere". At the same time, it has dramatically misused the way banks operate. Previously, basic banking activities such as account holder records, deposits, transactions, ledger record keeping, customer information, loan accounts, etc. were done in person.

Now, copy transactions, calculating, compiling customer information and maintaining a large website is likely with software that creates routine copy on a digital backend website. And the same software is integrated into all multi-branch banking systems, making the bank's major bank network.

One of the main purposes of this new technology is to make informed decisions with the help of facts and statistics. The various systems of the central banking system enable banks to store data efficiently. All information and reports can be accessed quickly through the confirmation process and permit customers and employees to make informed decisions.

In addition, it assists in producing and providing official and regulatory reports to government regulators. In addition, the core banking software offers customization.

In easy terms, core banking is an automated banking system that aims to provide complete bookkeeping methods, improved customer service and easy choice making. When all these important goals are achieve, it ultimately lead to amplified competence, customer satisfaction, and productivity.

ADVANTAGES OF CORE BANKING

The core banking systems have brought about a significant breakdown in the average person's operating system. When it comes to E-banking, it not only saves precious time for the average person but also makes it harder to work on his or her time. Moreover, reconciliation between branches has proved to be quick and easy.

The introduction of new products and information stored in the branch offices of various banks will become easier and easier as new branches now have greater access to the core areas of the country.

The speed and the large number of rapid technological advances and its impact on banking system solutions provide great relief. The functions of banking systems such as passport keeping, interest accounting and other bookkeeping records are kept aside because they can be done correctly and quickly.

1. Inadequate expert manpower should be used more efficiently.
2. Customers may bank from anyplace, making it more convenient.

3. Access to ATMs, Interest Banking, Mobile Banking, and Payment Gateways, among other services.
4. A more robust and cost-effective management information system.
5. A reduction in the number of people working in the branch.
6. Marketing, recovery, and personalised banking can all benefit from more staff.
7. Information is available in real time for decision-making.
8. Policies are carried out in a timely and accurate manner.
9. Improvements in the recovery process result in lower recovery costs and NPA supply.
10. Inter Branch Reconciliation; for example, has resulted in a reduction in manpower at Head Office as a result of innovative, redefined, or enhanced processes.
11. There has been a decrease in software maintenance at both the branch and the headquarters.
12. Reduced capital and revenue spend on printing and backup devices and media at branches due to centralized printing and backup.
13. Interactions with other financial institutions via electronic transactions.
14. Increased productivity leads to increased business prospects and cost savings.

The acceptance of basic banking systems has benefited banking and financial firms greatly. Customers, on the other hand, are equally pleased with technical services. Banking has become an important element of banks' daily operations and provides valuable support.

Remove the necessity for tedious and pointless tasks. With the development of an automated banking system, evaluating, maintaining, and upgrading data has become considerably easier. At the same time, it has improved worker productivity and competency. Now is the time to put your strength and abilities to good use.

The management of the information system can be done for low cost using major financial services. Makes quick decisions and provides quick access to information. New systems are more precise and limit the possibility of human error.

Branches with fewer employees and more potential for fraud. Additionally, it allows employees to deepen their customer relationships. In the end, it allows the bank to maintain a healthy customer base.

This approach has given users the option of banking anywhere and at any time. Major banking services are significantly simpler and easier to use than traditional banking systems.

Customers are not required to visit their bank office each time they require basic banking services. Mobile banking, internet banking, and ATMs are among the more easily available stations they now offer.

Rapidly and in real time, new information is available. Finally, it includes a list of available banking products that may be found virtually anyplace. Basic banking is straightforward, time-saving, and inexpensive, and it makes monitoring easier.

DISADVANTAGES OF CORE BANKING SOLUTION

Extreme dependence on technology

The strike on computer systems can cause the entire network to crash

If the data is not properly protected and if not properly maintained, cyber criminals can access sensitive data

Low flexibility

Essential banking systems are lithe, but to a sure extent. This income that their functionality can be comprehensive but requires a lot of money. The oldest software used today by banks is based on the COBOL language and few programmers are experts in that knowledge.

Insufficient scalability

When the first banking software was industrial, banks operate differently. They had fewer customers, less data processed and online banking was the prospect. Therefore, older software does not meet the rising needs. The decline of system supplies makes banks look for new solution.

High maintenance costs

The banking systems are exclusive to preserve (technical credit). On other hand, professionals needed (due to niche technology). On the other hand, every effort to extend system performance includes elevated costs and risks. The reason is the need to create customized solutions that are compatible with accessible ones.

CONCLUSION:

Over the existence, the core banking software continues to perform its function of providing efficient customer service. The figure of errors is small as the majorities tasks are perform by computers. In adding, banks can expand the use of used software and compete efficiently in the current market.

Facilitated decision-making process

The central banking system helps to bring together and analyze information which is the reason for the decision-making process quickly. This helps not only to evaluate customer requests quickly (e.g. about loans or debt), also decisions regarding banking growth guidelines, as well as entry into another, foreign brand.

E-BANKING EVOLUTION

Projects of the current state of affairs where E-banking is determining the monetary services industry.

A short history and study of the evolution of the E-banking industry worldwide using textual analysis reveals major barriers,

barriers and boosters to rapidly change the banking sector and the use of E-banking.

E-banking in India: The Reserve Bank of India forms a working group with Electronic Banking. The group categorized Electronic Banking products in India into 3 types based on the access levels provided. Of course:

- Information-Only System: The bank's website provides general information such as interest rates, branch locations, bank products and their features, and loan and deposit calculations.
- Electronic Information Transfer System (EITS): This system delivers account balances, transaction details, and a statement of accounts to customers.
- Fully Electronic Transactional System: This system is capable of bidirectional communication. The customer can submit transactions for online updating. This technology necessitates a high level of security and control.

Automated Teller Machines (ATM)

The ATM is intended to serve the most important banking function. It works with a plastic card that has unique characteristics. The check, customer presence, banking hour constraints, and paper confirmation are all replaced by the plastic card. Debit cards are available. Electronic Wallet Transfer (EWT) is launched from ATMs.

Credit and debit cards are accepted.

Within the limits specified by his or her bank, the Credit Card Owner is free to use his or her Credit Card whenever and whenever he or she likes. A prepaid card is a credit card. A Debit Card, on the other hand, is a fixed-amount prepaid card. When a customer uses this card, money is moved from the consumer's bank to the Internet Banking house's account. The accurate purchase price is subtracted from the customer account.

To improve security, smart card banks inserted chips to their existing magnetic cards.

Services for Bill Payment

As each bank has partnerships with different companies, service is available nationwide. Can pay power and telephone bills, mobile phones, credit cards, and premium insurance loans.

Transferring Money

This is wonderful and would pique the curiosity of every amam janta. Indian Railways has partnered with ICICI Bank, and you can now book your local train tickets online. The pass will be delivered to your door. However, the centre is only open to residents of Mumbai, Thane, Nashik, Surat, and Pune.

Passport for Trains

This is something that all amam janta are interested in. Indian Railways has partnered with ICICI Bank, and you can now book your local train tickets online. The pass will be delivered to your door.

Internet Banking for Investing

Online money transfers can be used to open an FD. Investors with a demat account linked to a bank account can now trade in the stock market with ease, and the cash will be credited to their bank account.

How to Recharge a Prepaid Phone

Fill out your prepaid mobile cards by sorting into internet banking for the time being. Simply select the operator's name, enter your phone number, and the charge number, and your phone will be ready in minutes.

Shopping

The list of all types of things, which may be purchased online, and the total is easily transferred from one account to another. The user can also book a train or an airline ticket.

Meaning E-banking:

Electronic banking is one of the most widely distributed Ecommerce avatars in the world. E-banking means electronic banking. It's similar to an E-business in the banking industry. E-banking is known "Virtual Banking" or "Online Banking". E-banking is the result of the growth expected by bank customers. E-banking involves banking based on information technology. Below this I.T. System, banking facilities are delivering through a Computerized System. The agenda involve straight message with customer.

The customer are not necessary to stay the bank building. Online banking can easily be defined as a system for entering into a sale by a particular customer and a bank using up to date equipment. With a variety of computer skills and other technological advances, online banking is one of the many businesses that have benefit from it. as banks play a very vital role in the national wealth, then there is a real require to get bigger and get better its features in order to more customer-friendly and accessible.

LEGAL FRAMEWORK FOR E BANK

In India bank largely regulated by the Banking Regulation Act, 1949, and the Reserve Bank of India Act in year 1934, and electronic records and systems are govern by the requirements controlled in the Information and Technology Act, 2000 as amended in 2008. The Internet. Banking is no separate business, it is a bank operated by electronic channels, and is simply an additional facility offered to banks. There are several laws governing internet banking in India. Some of those laws are: The Information Technology Act, 200, The Banking Regulation Act, 1949, Indian Contract Act, 1872, etc. Let's take a look at the provisions of all these major banking rules.

IT Act, 2000

(i) The IT Act, 2000 is the key law commerce with cybercrime and Electronic Commerce in India. This practice has a direct impact on the operation of online banking in India and therefore it can be argued that online banking cannot operate without compliance with the IT Act 2000. The following points highlight the importance of the Information Technology Act, 2000 regarding online banking:

(ii) **Scrutinization of Documents:**
Any bank transaction requires the processing and storage of various documents and in online banking these documents are kept and processed electronically. Official recognition of these electronic documents is provided by IT Act only

(iii) **Electronic Transaction:**
All transactions entered electronically are monitored through the provision of IT Act. Sections 10-A 17 of the Act provide for the legalization and enforcement of electronic transaction, and thus without the provisions of the IT Act no online banking business may challenged in a court of law.

(iv) **Authentication:**
Verification of electronic records for the purpose electronic banking must be accompanied by the provision of this act

viii) **Digital Signature:**
If the documents are digitally signed they are governed by the provisions of this Act only. Therefore, this action may be sufficient for the purpose of signing a document for online banking purposes.

(v) **Privacy:**
Privacy is very important in online banking because if privacy and security were not available, online banking would probably not have survived.

(vi) **Data theft:**
Section 66 of the IT Act penalizes a number of computer-related theft activities, a number of potential data theft

methods such as: hacking, launching and distributing viruses through computer networks, etc.

(vii) The purpose of the IT Act is to ease e-commerce and e-governance which are very important for the performance of Internet banking in India.

Few of the important provisions of the IT Act are as follows:-

a) **Section 3(2):** This section recognizes only one particular technology (crypto utility and confusion function) a earnings of authenticate electronic records. The approach is been kept technology neutral in various nations.

b) **Section 4:** This provision gives legal recognition to all the contracts and agreements made in electronic form.

c) **Section 72:** It provides for the penalty in case of privacy breach

d) **Section 79:** It provides immunity to the network service providers and excludes them from liability in case of any illegal activity committed through their network

In January 2011, RBI constituted G Gopalakrishna Working Group to review the security of Electronic Banking in India. The committee on April 2011 notified few changes which constitute the current regulatory guidelines.

2. Indian Payment Code, 1860

Many online Banking-related crimes are punished by the Indian Penal Code. There are various IPC provisions that protect next to Internet Banking fraud, theft, etc. Surprisingly there are a number of provisions in the Indian Penal Code that violate the IT Act, 2000. A few of those provisions are discussed below:

1. Data Theft: As defined in Section 378 of the IPC, theft includes the theft of data online or otherwise. There are a number of ways in which online banking data can be stolen for example: hijacking, virus transmission, computer damage, denial of access to an authorized person. Data protection

therefore becomes important. And IPC barriers such activities protect the interests of online banking users. Section 42421 of the IPC also prohibits data theft in India by punishing a person who assists or hides data.

2. Receipt of stolen property: If any person is found to have any further stolen property in an online banking business, he / she will be charged with IP s / 41122 and will be liable to imprisonment for 3 months or a fine or both. This provision of the IPC is similar to Section 66-B of the IT Act,
3. Cheating: Section 411 (Fraudulent acquisition of stolen property) of the IPC provides for punishment for any act committed by fraud. Section 66-C 23 of the IT Act also penalizes the same. Anyone committing a computer cheating is said to be committing Cheating by Personation.
4. Evil: unnecessary to say, anyone who, with hateful intent, infects a computer program corrupts a computer program, or refuses to access a person authorized to use that system, will be charged with malicious misconduct. and a penalty under Section 425 of the IPC for imprisonment for a period of up to 3 months or on a fine or both.
5. Fraud: In Internet Banking Transactions fraud can be dedicated by providing false electronic documents or other records.

There are a number of other criminal activities which the IPC doesn't punish, but are punishable under the IT Act. Few of them are:

1. The IPC does not penalize a person who charges for services rendered to another person's account by disrupting or hacking any computer system, or computer network. Such action is punishable by / s 43 (h) of the IT Act.
2. Disruption of computer source document. To some extent he is punished with / s 409 of the IPC but it is not very detailed there. Section 65 of the IT Act therefore addresses this issue.

3. Violations of Security / Privacy while trading online: You are penalized in / s 66E of IT Act. Privacy while logging, entering a password, trading, is very important in Internet Banking.
4. Preservation of Mediators (Banks for us): Section 67 requires a 'mediator' to maintain and maintain all such information determined by the central government. The ordinance was challenged in court in the case of Shreya Singhal, in which case the court affirmed the legitimacy of this section.

1. Other Legislations

1. Income tax 1961: Section 40A(3): The benefits of this section are available to the account holder only if the amount is transferred via online banking or check. This section aims to prevent tax evasion and to make all transactions more than 20000 under the pre-bank preview.

2. NEGOTIABLE INSTRUMENT ACT, 1881: Section 6: The concept of Abbreviated Check and e-check added. These checks are non-negotiable electronic format tools that are part of online banking. All of these tools are needed to maintain minimum security requirements through the use of a digital signature (which can be biometric).

2. PREVENTION OF MONEY LAUNDERING ACT, 2002: Section 11: It places a duty on all financial institutions and the coordinator to keep a record of all transactions. This applies to all banks whether they provide physical or online services. This offer helps prevent money laundering from happening through online banking.

4. CONSUMER PROTECTION ACT, 1986: This action is intended to protect the interests of consumers. It also applies to Banking services. Issues such as privacy, confidentiality of consumer civil rights and liability of consumers and banks, etc. in the case online banking they are protected by this action.

IMPACT OF INTERNET BANKING

Internet Banking is much cheaper in comparison virtual banking services. Setting up online banking is cheaper compared to banks, and therefore, leads to the introduction of many new methods in the world of banking. The Traditional Banking System may find it difficult to raise extra money or investments in the Stock Market, but this, unlike Online Banking, seems to be a much easier task to deal with investment. Internet Banking is now an significant part of the global monetary market, in order to meet the needs of different financial markets / institutions. Accordingly Internet Banking has rightly had a strong impact on global and domestic markets, and its popularity has grown exponentially as internet users have expanded globally.

Internet Banking gives Advantages to the Customers

• From Banking Institution's Point of View

1. Reduce the cost of delivering services
2. Gives a cutthroat advantage to the banks from their peers
3. Promotional Advertisements on their site may also produce some additional revenue
4. Paperless transactions
5. Increase in Investments, as the customers can apply for loans electronically without visiting the banks.

• From Customer's Point of View:

1. 24 x 7 access to the banking services
2. Access to the account activity in a very quick time
3. Application for loans, ATM Cards, etc
4. Home based transfer of funds, payment for purchasing something online, etc.

•

MODULE-3

ELECTRONIC DELIVERY CHANNELS

TELLER COUNTERS:

To make easy rapid business, banks gives teller counters to get out money from the put account.

There are two types of teller counters

a) Manual teller counter; and

b) Automatic teller counter

In physical calculations banks often permit for withdrawals from savings accounts. A check or withdrawal form is delivered over the counter and payment is made after verify equilibrium in the account, as well as sample count of the account manager's signature.

At the default calculation ATMs are set up to grip money dealings 24 hours with no a break. There is no requiring employing anyone to confirm the sense of balance, compare template signature or give or take cash. Let's learn how an ATM machine works.

When a bank installs ATMs, it provides a magnetic card and a secret code number to all account holders. This code number is called a Personal Identification Number (PIN). If the cardholder wants to withdraw or deposit money, he or she must first identify himself or herself in order to use the ATM according to his or her PIN. When you place an ATM card into the machine, it prompts you for a PIN. The PIN can be entered by tapping the machine screen or using the keyboard.

Money can be deposited or withdrawn in line with the machine's instructions once your identity has been verified. It is necessary to retain cash in a particular envelope supplied at the ATM in order to deposit it. The envelope will be kept near to the edge after closing it and writing the relevant information on it. The envelope will be automatically put into the machine when you hit the deposit button.

Officials from the bank will periodically collect the envelope and deposit the funds into the relevant accounts.

Likewise, withdrawals can be complete by vital or tapping the removal button and specifying the quantity necessary. The precise quantity of cash will be obtainable to you as soon as you leave.

CASH DISPENSER

A cash dispenser is a machine that allows people to withdraw money from their bank account using a certain card.

The host processor deducts the desired amount from the cardholder's account when the cardholder demands cash. Once the money has been sent from the customer's account to the processor's bank account, the processor sends the approval code to the ATM and the allowed machine to withdraw the cash.

ATM

Automated teller machine (ATM) is the abbreviation for automated teller machine. It's an electronic machine that can only be used by bank customers to conduct transactions. Users receive access to their accounts by utilising a certain sort of plastic card that has their personal information magnetically encoded on it. On this line, the signal code is sent to the central bank via modem.

Users use the card to obtain access to their accounts and make transactions by inserting it into ATMs.

Automated Teller Machine (ATM)?

By using an automatic teller machine or ATM we can make various financial transactions such as deposits, withdrawals, transfers, account details, ATM PIN exchanges, and link Aadhaar number and bank account for communication between employees. Bankers and customer can be reduced.

A consumer can do simple transactions without the help of a bank employee by using an automated teller machine (ATM) or an automated banking machine (ABM). ATMs are classified into two groups. The consumer can only withdraw money from the basic account and receive a statement of account balance. Another sophisticated deposit processing system that accepts credit cards and generates account summaries.

History of Automated Teller Machines

The first concept of ATMs came from different countries such as Japan, UK, Sweden & US. Thus, Japan introduced a Computer Borrowing Machine called a computer loading machine to provide cash.

Following some progress, the first cash machine was invented by Britain, in London, in 1967. The development of ATMs was slow because it was introduced in the early 1990s to Indians and aided by foreign banks.

When many banks faced major problems due to the lack of a strong branch system, cash machines emerged as the best solution to these problems. Customers by providing luxury services at minimal cost. Since then, many advances in technology have arrived and customer access has also improved with restrictions.

Diagram of Automated Teller Machine

Two input devices and four output devices are shown in the automated teller machine diagram. Card readers and keypads are examples of input devices, whereas speaker, display screen, receipt printer, and cash depositor are examples of output devices.

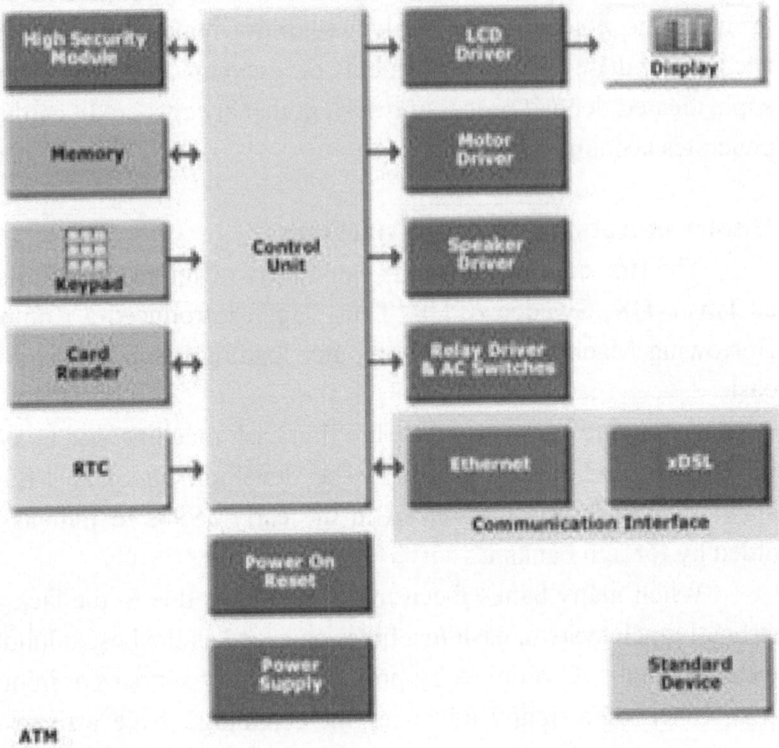

Input Devices

The input devices includes card reader and keypad.

Card Reader

Card reader is an input device which reads data from the card. The card reader is element of identify your account number and the magnetic strap on the back of the ATM card is used to commune with the card reader. The card swipe or is pressed into the card reader that records your account details i.e. the data from the card is transferred to the host browser (server). The hosting processor therefore uses this data to get information from cardholders.

Keypad

The card is familiar after the machine has requested additional information like your ID no, withdrawal, and question balance.

Every card has a different PIN so that it is less likely that someone will remove money from your account. There are different rules for protecting the PIN when sending it to the host browser. PIN is send most encrypted. The keyboard consists of 48 keys and is connected to the processor.

Output Devices

The output devices include speaker, display screen, receipt printer, and cash depositor.

Speaker

The speaker provides audio pointer when a particular key is pressed.

A computer monitor

The transaction information is displayed on the display screen. The display panel shows every step of the withdrawal process. The vast majority of ATMs employ a CRT or LCD display.

Printer for Receipts

The receipt printer prints all of the details of your withdrawal, including the date, time, and amount of withdrawal, as well as the balance of your account.

Dispenser of Cash

An ATM's spirit is embodied by a cash machine. This is an intermediary ATM system that receives the required cash. The user can collect money in this section. Each building must be calculated and the required amount provided by the money maker. If the money is collected in some situations, it will be transferred to a different group and become a reject bit. All of these measurements are carried out by high-precision sensors. The ATM keeps track of all transactions and keeps a comprehensive record.

ATM Networking

In ATMs, the Internet Service Provider (ISP) also plays an important role. This aids in the connection of ATMs and hosting processors. The cardholder enters the information when the transaction is completed. The ATM handling processor receives this information. This information is verified by the host with the approved bank. The hosting processor gives the authorization code to the machine for the money to be transmitted after the specifics are finalized.

Types of ATM Machines

There are different types of ATMs in the market which include the following. Most of the host processors can support either leased-line or dial-up machines

Leased Line ATM Machines

A four-wire point-to-point dedicated telephone line connects the leased line machines to the host CPU. In the workplace, these machines are preferred. These machines have an extremely high running cost.

Dial-Up ATM Machines

Dial-up ATMs connect to the host CPU via a modem and a regular phone connection. These require a standard connection and have a lower initial installation cost. When compared to leased line machines, these machines have a cheap running cost.

White Label ATM

These ATMs are arranged, operated & owned through non-bank entities. These ATMs were launched by RBI (Reserve Bank of India) for assisting financial insertion as well as drive ATM access within the country. These types of ATMs will not show any bank's logo. The first white logo ATM was launched by TATA in India.

Brown Label ATM

Brown label ATMs were maintained & owned through a service provider where a supporter bank whose brand can be employed on ATM to take care of network connectivity as well as cash organization

Onsite ATM

These ATM machines are arranged in locations wherever a bank branch is located. So, both the bank as well as ATM can be used physically for several purposes by being on-site. Many customers can utilize this to keep away from the queue lines at the branch of the bank so that time taken to finish their bank transactions can be reduced.

Offsite ATM

These machines are arranged on a separate, which means that the bank has a place where there is only an ATM machine then this becomes an offsite ATM. This can be complete to make sure that the bank reaches out to more environmental locations to utilize its services by the people even when there is no branch of the bank within the region. So these machines will operate outside of the bank locations.

Cash Dispenser

These machines permit simply balance inquiry, mini statement & cash withdrawals.

Mobile ATM

These machines move in the locations for the users because COVID 19 has led to the rush within the several Mobile ATMs.

Green Label

These types of ATMs are used especially for farming business.

Orange Label

These are mainly used for split business.

Yellow Label

These ATMs are used for an online purchase by providing an E-Commerce facility

Pink Label

These ATMs are used especially for women. These ATMs are observed by protectors to make sure that only women are accessing or not so that women waiting in long queues can be reduced.

ATM Security:

The ATM card is secured by a PIN that must be kept secret. There is no way to obtain your card's PIN. It is secured using well-designed software

Automated Teller Machine Working Principle

The automated teller machine is nothing more than a data terminal with two inputs and four outputs. The PC is connected to these devices. The ATM's heart is the computer. A unified database system underpins all of the ATMs available around the world. The ATM must connect to the host computer and communicate with it (server).

The internet service provider communicates with the host CPU (ISP). It is the entrance of all ATM networks available to the cardholder from side to side. When a cardholder wants to use an ATM, he or she enters the appropriate information into a card reader and keypad. This is forwarded to the host processor by the ATM. The transaction request is sent to the cardholder bank by the host processor.

If the cardholder requires cash, the host computer deducts funds from his or her account. After the monies have been transferred from the

How to Operate ATM Machine?

The automated teller machine is extremely simple to use. The pace-by-pace algorithm for ATM is detailed further down.

- Go to a nearby ATM and insert your ATM card into the machine.
- Select a language to appear on the ATM monitor, such as your native tongue, Hindi, or English.
- Choose a transaction type from a list of options such as money transfer, withdrawal, deposit, and so on.
- Select an account type, such as savings or current.
- Enter your 4-digit ATM pin number and the appropriate withdrawal amount.
- Gather your funds and keep your receipt.
- If you want to perform further transactions, you can do so by selecting the option.

ATM Software

The ATM (Automated Teller Machine) mean is a combination of hardware and software. The hardware of the machine is mostly proposed for deposits of cash, withdrawal, payments of credit card & for reporting the in order of account. The software of ATM is intended to control ATM business & channels on central database.

The famous ATM software that works on the XFS platform comprises Absolute INTERACT, KAL Kalignite Software Platform, Wincor Nixdorf ProTopas, Phoenix Interactive VISTAatm, Intertech inter-ATM & Euronet EFTS. Once the ATM machines were shifted to industry standards then anxiety has increased on the software stack of ATM.

ATM Charges

At present, everyone goes to ATM centers frequently for different purposes like to withdraw, deposit, mini statement, pin change, etc. But for the account holders, the transactions are not free from their bank ATM as well as other bank ATMs.

So for bank account holders, they permited for five free transactions from their ATMs and three times from other bank ATMs. The ATM transactions not only include withdrawal but also include changing PIN numbers, balance inquiries, mini statements, etc. It charges for when we withdraw the amount. When the number of transactions exceeds the fixed transactions like withdrawing/non-cash withdraw then it will charge some amount which is deducted from your account.

Every bank provides ATM cards for their bank account holders at the time of account opening without any charge. But, different banks will charge while using the ATMs for transactions when it exceeds a fixed number of transactions. For initial transactions, it will not charge for transactions. For instance, the top banks like SBI, ICICI, and HDFC will charge per transaction like the following.

- For SBI bank, the free transactions per month are five at SBI and three in other banks. The cost per each transaction is 25 rupees.
- For ICICI bank, free transactions at all ICICI banks & charges 25 rupees in non-ICICI bank ATMs
- For HDFC Bank, free five transactions at metro ATMs-3 whereas non-metro ATMs-5 and charges 20 plus rupees

Some Facts about ATMs in India

Some facts about an ATM in India are discussed below.

- As per 2019 records, the total ATM machines located are 222,318
- The highest number of ATMs used in Maharashtra, India.
- For SBI bank, the highest ATM machines were installed in India are 59,521.
- The first talking ATM in India is located in Ahmedabad Highest cash withdrawal limit in an ATM is 20k to 1 lack depending on the bank.

ATM Maintenance

The following five things must keep in mind while maintaining the ATM.

- Standard ATM parts must be cleaned
- The machine must be checked for inspecting
- Surveillance camera must be checked whether that is working or not
- ATM must be protected from the elements

Advantages

The **advantages of an automated teller machine** include following.

- Automated teller machines are easily arranged in different areas so that every bank customer can visit the machine to execute any transaction.
- used to take out the money in a part of minutes so that instance can be saved.
- To get an ATM card at present, process is hassle-free because no documentation work is required. All the banks are providing an ATM card at the instance of opportunity an account.
- ATM machines provide business details to be familiar with the stability of the account holder
- Utility payments can be done by using an ATM card
- ATMs provide twenty four hours seven days service
- ATM is much secured because it can be used only when the person knows the ATM password.
- ATMs will reduce the work pressure for the bank employees.
- It reduces the cash-carrying because anyone can withdraw the money at any ATM center so it works like a cash point
- The ATM provides 24 hours examine to the customers
- The ATM provides isolation in banking connections
- The ATM may give customer new money notes
- The ATMs are suitable for banks customers
- The ATM provide services without any mistake

Features

The following are some of the features of an automated teller machine.

- Transfer funds between connected bank accounts • ensure account stability • print new communication list • change your pin • deposit cash • prepaid cell recharge • bill payments • money removal
- In your faraway words, use a variety of attributes.

Disadvantages

The **disadvantages of automated teller machines** include the following.

- IT charges some amount once free transactions exceed
- Once ATM card damages then cash withdraw is not possible
- Possibility of cash robbery from ATMs
- ATM pin can be easily hacked by criminals by operating an ATM
- The risk of theft is high while going to ATMs

TELEPHONY

Telephony is the technology linked with message among two or more far-away party through the broadcast of electronic communication or additional information. For an extended time linked with voice announcement, the phone has evolved to include messaging, record calling, tape conferencing.

In fact, when talking about the phone, the cell phone acts as a two-way radio to transmit and receive radio signals from a local cell tower. Mobile chat happens when your phone converts sound waves into electrical signals and transmits them through radio waves to a nearby cellular network tower.

Telephony is a word that describes a knowledge that permits public to have long-distance voice communication.

Telephone exchange has in the past necessary the use of conventional wireless telephones, portable devices consisting of both speakers (transmitters) and receivers linked to local exchange networks via portable cables. Telecommunications are becoming increasingly common with the use of modern computer and mobile technology, thus narrowing the line between the telephone and telecommunications sectors. The description of the phone and its width has grown accordingly.

How telephony works

- The operation of a typical telephone. A flexible telephone system cuts across the sphere, converting the noise impact at the end of a wire into an electric signal for their purpose via PSTN connections. The forwarding is then converted to audio signals by the receiving phone, allowing for real-time communication.
- How the mobile phone works. Using cell phone technology, the cell phone convert sound into electrical signals transmitted by radio waves to a local cell tower. The mobile network uses radio signals to transmit this information to the recipient's phone, which, in turn, converts the signal back to sound.

IP Fax also called as Fax over IP or virtual fax, works as a standard fax but over the Internet. The software inserts the code into a scan file and converts it into data that can travel over local or wide local IP network before being recorded or converted and finally received.

Telephony platforms and vendors

- From big carriers to up-and-coming startups, businesses may now pick from a myriad of on-premises and cloud-based VoIP telephony solutions. The following are some of them:
- Cisco Webex
- Google
- Microsoft
- Nextiva
- RingCentral
- Verizon

INTERNET

Customers can usually access their accounts through the internet at traditional banks and credit unions with branches.

However, mobile access is mostly provided through online banks and providers. You won't be able to speak with a banker face to face, but you can access your account at any moment using a mobile device or computer.

The Internet is **enormous system that connect computer all over the globe**. Through the Internet, people can share in order and commune from wherever with an Internet connection.

Internet banking allows customers to conduct financial transactions from anywhere, at any time, via the internet. It allows customers to conduct all normal transactions at any time and from any location, at no cost, and without having to physically visit a bank, internet banking offers.

A bank user can use any internet-enabled device, such as a laptop, desktop computer, or mobile phone, to access net banking. They do not need to go to the bank to transfer money from one account to another, check their transaction statement, or ask questions about banking transactions.

Benefits of online banking

There are other advantages to banking online, in addition to the ability to bank at any time and from any location. It's also possible that you'll be able to:

Pay bills online

- One of the biggest benefits of online banking is that you don't have to leave your day to go to the bank. You can just log into your account and pay off your debt right away. If you have monthly payments to or from retailers, you can also set up automated billing payments to boost efficiency. This will help you manage your cash flow. Money transfer
- Instead of travelling to the bank and waiting in line, you might be able to check online in minutes. Most financial institutions offer mobile apps that mimic their services, so you can bank on the go. Furthermore, some banks provide

customer service 24 hours a day, seven days a week, allowing you to reach them at any time.

- If your firm uses online banking, you can cut your banking expenditures in half.

Speed and Efficiency

- If you need to transfer money, apply for a new loan, or do almost any other type of bank transaction, you will almost always have to wait in line at a physical bank. With internet banking, there's no need to wait. As long as you can log in, you may check your accounts, get a new credit card, and do practically any banking you want without having to go to the bank or wait in line

Disadvantages of Online Banking

There is no such thing as the best bank for anything. Despite their numerous benefits, there are certain disadvantages to utilising online banks. The following are some of the drawbacks of dealing with an online bank:

Technology Issues

If you visit a physical bank, you can develop a relationship with a teller over time. When dealing with internet banking, on the other hand, you're frequently referred to an anonymous customer support representative who may be familiar with the next customer. If you're really strapped for cash, having a relationship with someone who can assist you and knows you well might be a huge benefit over a solid internet banking relationship.

Security Issues

Online banks can transfer money between accounts and pay off bills, but if you have sophisticated operations, you may prefer international banks with bricks and mortar locations. Business-focused banks, such as Chase, have the potential to conduct global operations, similar to how online banks can send payments in more than 35 different currencies throughout the world. Many online banks are unable to provide private, visitable, and necessary public services to the most crucial financial services, such as property buying, since they lack a physical presence.

Inefficient at Complex Transactions

Although most online banks have a good reputation and are reliable, it might be difficult to trust a bank that has real assets, especially when dealing with large sums of money. What happens to your funds if a website goes down unexpectedly? You run the risk of identity theft - or real theft - if someone gains unauthorised access to your account using a stolen or stolen password or login data.

No Relationship with Personal Banker

In many ways, an online banking system is as good as your — or their — internet connection. You may be unable to access your account if the power goes out or the servers go down. Although some banks provide a customer care phone number, it may be inconvenient if Internet connectivity is disrupted. You can always find someone to talk to at a real bank's branch.

Inconvenient to Make Deposits

It may seem odd that a bank whose goal is to recruit consumers makes it difficult for them to deposit money, yet this may be the case with some online banks. You can't just reduce the amount of money or check the local branch with internet banking. Some online banks, such as Ally Bank, will even refuse to approve any investment. To make a deposit at Ally Bank, for example, you must write a check, transfer money to another bank or account, or utilise a bank e-check service. **Mobile** banking is a service provided by a bank or other financial institution that allows its customers to perform remote monetary dealings using mobile banking the act performing monetary dealings on mobile phones (mobile phone, tablet, etc.).

This job can be as easy as a fraudulent banking transaction or transactional service or be as complex as a customer paying bills or sending money abroad.

Benefits of Mobile Banking

1. The mobile phone can always be or remain portable due to the natural design, permiting users to participate in activities such as travel or socializing, while transactions on mobile devices are made online.
2. **Location-centric-**Not only are cell phones ubiquitous, but a Global Positioning System (GPS) can be developed to identify them and attempt to personalise them based on existing services? The ability to determine the location of internet users provides a unique benefit of mobile trading via online trading. Mobile commerce providers will be able to locate and transfer information locally utilising this technology.
3. Access to electronic services is not limited by time or location for some people. People stuck in traffic or in queue, for example, will be able to use mobile marketing apps to purchase their favourite online activities or manage their daily activities. Consumers can enjoy unique indulgences that enhance their quality of life. The customer will be more dependable if the services are more comfy. As a result, social networking sites with mobile marketing apps are now available to provide convenience.
4. Customization - The impact of a cell phone is significantly greater than that of a personal computer. As a result, mobile device manufacturers are building the oldest and most customizable lifestyle tool. For example, more targeted advertising could be achieved by combining statistical data acquired by cellular service providers with current location information for mobile customers. Advertising messages can be tailored based on the information provided, as well as the original or previous consumers' purchase patterns. 5.

Identification capabilities - The mobile phone enables secure mobile transactions in an environment where personal computers are virtually anonymous (no name). One person always utilizes mobile devices and is ready for targeted marketing; service providers can easily identify the user using Global Positioning System (GPS) technology. and there you have it

TRADITIONAL BANKING PRODUCTS

Traditional banks permit you to build relationships with their employees. Traditional banking can also provide you with a variety of services that you will not be able to access via mobile banking. Items such as mortgages, loans, various types of insurance, and investment services are currently only available through traditional banks.

The traditional bank has its head office, as well as regional HQs, with branches located in all the countries in which it operates. Many traditional banks use their name ATMs. Small traditional banks may come jointly to use big numbers to share costs.

Traditional bank product "means a loan, discount, deposit, or trust service. National banks, subsidiary banks, and corporate branches and foreign banking agencies must comply with anti-bond obligations.

NEW BANKING PRODUCTS

Savings account

A checking account may be the first thing that comes to mind when considering what banks have to offer. This common account type allows you to save and control the money you spend on a daily basis. Once your account has been suspended, you can pay for anything with a debit card or a check, which will deduct funds directly from your account. Using your bank card and PIN, the unique password you choose to safeguard your account, you can also get cash at an ATM or branch.

A savings account can help you separate the amount you want to save from the amount you need to use. For many, it is an easy way to work toward a specific goal, such as saving for home improvement or building an emergency fund. Most savings accounts can automatically transfer money from your test account to your savings account every month, so you don't even have to consider doing it yourself. An added bonus is that banks usually pay interest on savings accounts. That is free money that can help you reach your financial goals faster.

Money Market Accounts (MMAs) are a type of savings account that provides higher interest rates than traditional savings accounts. You will be able to gain more if you put in more effort. However, keep in mind that owing to organisational restrictions, you will only be able to make up to six withdrawals every month.

Certificate of Deposit.

A CD is a type of bank account in which you agree to keep your money in the account for a period of time, from 6 months to 5 years.

Debit card

With a debit card, you can pay for your daily expenses with just a swipe (and usually with your PIN). The money will come directly from your checking account so there is no need to carry cash if you do not like it. Also, if your debit card is lost or stolen, you will not be liable for unauthorized purchases if you report it in time. Loss of money, unfortunately, is often lost forever.

Credit card

Allows you to pay for items with a credit line. In fact, you borrow money and then pay back what you owe. But keep in mind that different credit cards charge different interest rates, so it's important to know what you agree with (so you don't end up paying too much over time). Another way to avoid paying interest is to pay off your debt in full every month. You may also want to be aware of annual payments, especially if it is a card with benefits such as mileage or refund. Buying a credit card without annual fees is always an option.

SEGEMENTATION

The three main categories of business banking are retail banks, central banks, and asset management.

Market segregation processes permit banks to focus on catering to the multiple needs of a particular group of customers. The ability of banks to know and know the level of wants and interests of their customers is important and beneficial in changing, and shaping the portfolio of a company product (service).

Retail Banking Segment

Retail banks are the main donors. It is a feature most people are recognizable with, as it covers activities that take place at a bank branch. The products involved in the retail bank comprise deposits, credit cards, and real estate loans. This section is also known as a private bank, as it assists individuals. However, it is also under attack at smaller retail customers.

Revenue from commercial banks is divided into interest and non-interest. Interest income includes about 70% of sales revenue. It is calculated by taking interest collected on mortgage and credit cards and deducting interest paid on deposits.

Interest-free income accounts for about 30% of the revenues of the retail bank. It is calculated from taking the difference between all non-interest incomes and operating expenses.

Revenue is generated from account funds, operating expenses, credit card funds, and foreign exchange earnings. The fees are usually small and the customers do not see it. The costs included in this section are compensation costs and infrastructure costs. They can add up to 50% of the bank's sales revenue

Wholesale Banking Segment

The world's second-largest bank is wholesale banking. Markets for wholesale banking are sometimes known as wholesale banking markets. Markets for Capital the exchange mechanism that sends money to investors who want to lend their extra money to businesses is known as big markets.

This sector is linked with the bank and deals with corporate customer and institutions. Investment banks serve as intermediaries.

Corporate lending, sales, and trading are some of the responsibilities. S&T is an investment banking team that consists of traders who invite institutional investors with ideas and possibilities, as well as traders who place orders and advise customers on financial entry and exit. positions.

Purchase Accounting - Megers & Acquisitions is the lifeblood of a collateral firm, and acquisition of Purchase Accounting - Megers & Acquisitions is the lifeblood of a collateral firm (M&A) Accounting for acquisitions and acquisitions will be covered in this guide. A firm buys property, undisclosed business parts, or companies owned by another company in a transaction. A group of companies buys another firm as a whole.

The big banking sector typically accounts for 15% to 40% of overall income. This is heavily influenced by banking and market conditions. This is the most difficult component to forecast, and it often has the highest value for low duplication. Market changes and a lack of employment disclosure make it impossible to estimate revenue. Trading is a flexible activity that represents 30 - 40% of total revenue.

Revenue arises from profits and losses arising from non-performing investments in fixed income investments, funds, assets, and budgets. Other functions in this segment are integration and acquisition. There are huge benefits, as there are no financial requirements. Revenue depends on payments, which are usually between 0.15 to 1.5% of total work.

Wealth Management Segment

Wealth management is a fast-growing segment of banks. Revenue is generated by brokerage and asset management services. Asset management is often regarded as the highest value of most Comps - Comparable Trading Multiples Analyzing similar trading multipliers (Comps) involves analyzing companies with similar operating, financial and ownership profiles to provide useful insights into: performance, finance, growth rates, margin styles, spending big money. repetitive measurement, DCF speculation, and IPO benchmarks have more segments for a number of reasons.

It has additional benefits due to lower debt requirements; there is low flexibility, and high growth. Growth is caused by changes in demographics.

In terms of revenue, as most of the assets are invested in Equity In finance, equal to the market value of the assets held by shareholders after all debts have been settled. In the financial statements, equity refers to the share price of shareholders in the balance sheet, which is equal to the assets excluded liabilities. The term, "equity", in finance and accounting, conveys the idea of fair and equitable management, and commissions of commerce contribute to revenue.

There has been more trading activity in recent years, increasing commissions. However, the temporary increase in trading profits is a major source of volatility due to dependence on equity markets. On the other hand, since management-related costs do not depend on market presentation, instability does not grow.

Advisors who can build and manage strong relationships with wealthy customer are very significant in the wealth management phase. Since both trading commissions and management fees depend on the number of customer, it is important to hire consultants who can achieve customer goals. Strong relations also mean that customers are less likely to leave during the market downturn. It is advisable to reassure customers that they will continue to trust the bank even if the markets are not performing well.

ELECTRONIC MONEY

Electronic money is money that is stored in computer banking systems. Electronic money is backed by fiat currency, which separates it from cryptocurrency. Various companies permit electronic transactions to be made, such as Square or PayPal.

In the last few decades, the total amount of electronic money can be verified in a variety of sources, including India. It was not long before the Government of India announced a reduction in its spending to make the nation a safer economy.

To facilitate transactions from bank accounts, financial firms and banks sign agreements with e-money networking processors to give customers access to smart cards that they will be able to trade electronically with.

Also, as most e-commerce platforms permit e-money transactions, consumers are now able to purchase almost all the goods and services available online.

Why is Electronic Money Important?

Due to major advances in technology; digital transactions with smart cards, digital wallets, and mobile wallets have been on the rise among consumers.

Also, as the statement of demon possession in India, the use of tangible money in doing so has declined. Properly managed, the use of electronic money has great potential to encourage non-financial transactions in the country.

However, electronic money is often criticized for its risks and risks. as transactions are processed through computer systems, there may be situations where electronic transactions may not be possible due to a system error.

Also, since electronic devices do not require physical authentication to transmit from one person to another, the potential for fraudulent activities is high.

How can E-Money be Used

A detailed rulebook on EMD2 makes it clear that e-money should be used. Therefore, it can find use in transactional transactions similar to that of cash. E-money can serve as payment for goods and services as long as their suppliers accept electronic payments.

Software-based e-money products may seem like a "normal" way of spending e-money these days. By taking this form, our electronic money is stored and transferred digitally through software running on personal computers, tablets or smartphones. With that amount of money, we can make our payment electronically (or e-payment), using an e-wallet provider (such as PayPal). Naturally, all of this requires an internet connection and a remote server.

Hardware-based e-money products do not require an internet connection. Instead, the amount of money lies in a real device called a hardware wallet (i.e., a chip card or prepaid mobile app). Addition and withdrawal usually takes place through a special device reader, while payment usually takes place in a visible sales area. In any case, however, e-money transactions, based on hardware and software-based, should not involve banks to pay, as long as it is a certified e-money service that operates the service in question.

What are the Benefits of E-Money?

E-money has dramatically lessened the significance of cash in our digital age – and in some countries, it may even replace it totally at some point in the future. The many advantageous aspects of e-money, for companies, financial institutions, and customers alike, are the driving force behind this transformation. a choice of:

1. Security

Many experts consider e-money to be far more secure than cash. You may not be able to interpret or provide additional information due to a statistical error. And criminals cannot steal so easily. Encryption technology, customer authentication technology (such as multi-item authentication) and control standards ensure that electronic money is also kept secure on the web. To prevent identity theft and other computer crimes related to your e-money wallet, service providers are also responsible for KYC compliance, anti-fraud, risk management and compliance with AML.

2. Convenience

Online payments have become the backbone of electronic money - and with good reason. Choosing to pay in advance with a bank payment method as an online payment method ends with a trip to your bank branches or your ever-changing banking platform. If you select a debit or credit / debit card as an online payment method, you must enter your credit card details or bank account details each time you pay online.

E-money service providers provide e-wallets where you can store data for your payment instrument. To pay online, simply select your e-wallet as payment method and purchase with just 1 click. It's like opening your wallet and giving cash, without digital.

3. Fast Transactions

The third quality that speaks to e-money is its speed of production. Electronic money making in real estate or online store happens instantly. Online money transfers between taxpayer and payroll accounts continue much faster than wireless transfers - it is a matter of minutes rather than a few days.

What are the Disadvantages of E-Money?

All benefits aside, electronic money has its own risks and drawbacks other forms of money such as cash do not suffer from as strongly.

1. High Security Requirements

A high level of electronic money security is linked to a drop, necessitating further support for e-wallet providers. Electronic money does not pass hands; instead, it is transferred from one account to another. You do not need to be present to pay online, but your e-money payment provider must follow security protocols. As a result, service providers must adhere to the KYC and dynamic processes required by PSD2 at all costs and with every effort. Anti-fraud and anti-money laundering policies are in the same boat. Finally, corporations may ask customer to give extra unpaid data, such as service bills, copies of ID cards, or personal identification verification during video conversations, depending on the transaction's value

2. Not Always Available

It is not just a question of infrastructure, but also of opportunity, whether or not you have access to e-money payment services. Many countries offer electronic processing of e-money services. However, the EMI emission is dangerous in any circumstance, for example, due to faults or political interference. In addition, depending on the location, installation may be less safe when it comes to internet connectivity or the availability of online e-commerce services or mobile trade sites. Finally, it is dependent on the seller in question; sellers should include an e-wallet provider for their customers. PayPal electronic payments, for example, cannot be used for merchants who are solely affiliated with hello Pay.

In a nutshell, e-cash, often known as electronic cash, is a digital money product that allows people to pay for goods and services without having to use paper or coin money. A digitally encoded card was used to replace paper money in the offline version of e-cash.

Prepaid electronic tokens include digital currency, debit cards, and electronic cases, whereas postpaid electronic tokens include electronic checks and credit cards. Cash that is digital (electronic). Cardholders using credit or debit cards can also make payments with their credit or debit cards.

Electronic cash is a form of payment that is exchanged electronically. Customers withdraw electronic coins from a bank and pay merchants with them. The merchants deposit the coins to the bank. This scheme involves computers networks over which the payment is made.

ELECTRONIC CASH PAYMENT

1. E-cash is an electronic payment system in which a predetermined amount of money is saved on a customer's device and made available for online transactions. A stored-value card is one that has a certain amount of money on it that may be used to make a purchase in the issuer's store.
2. Credit cards, debit cards, virtual cards, and ACH are the most popular electronic payment methods (direct deposit, direct debit, and electronic checks).
3. The following is a diagram of how internet payment processing works:
4. The customer selects an item and takes out their credit card.
5. A transaction is submitted by the merchant.
6. The payment entry delivers the transaction to the processor in a secure manner.
7. The transaction is verified and approved by the processor.
8. The processor receives funds from the customer's bank.

Types of payments

- Cash (bills and change): Cash is one of the most common methods of payment....
- Personal Cheque (US check): These are prepared using the buyer's account information.
- Debit Card: Using a debit card, money is taken immediately from the buyer's account.
- Credit Card: Credit cards resemble debit cards in appearance.

MODULE-4
ELECTRONIC DELIVERY PRODUCTS

Delivery channels include branches; field workers; ATMs; payment points; merchandise; moving branches; cell phones; and online banking.

Online banking permits the user to perform online monetary business. Online bank is also recognized as online banking or web banking. Online banking provides customers all types of facilities typically all obtainable through the local branch which include deposits money , transfers, and online payment .

Bank branches constitute a standard route for banking services. About each bank in the globe have twigs even though the existing banks have condensed dependence on these kindling and trying to restore classy twigs with less expensive technology.

At present, however, branches are still single of the majority trendy ways to deliver banking services since they permit banks to provide all the services in one place. As well, the size of bank branches, in conditions of residences, has declined significantly over the long-ago few existence. This is due to technical innovations that have made it possible for improved storage and dispensation without the use of any room. Technology has affected the entire banking sector and this includes conventional model such as bank twigs.

Modern Delivery Formats

Current methods of examine release are very dissimilar from branch-based model. The primary is just to center on effectiveness. This wealth that banks intend to provide additional services at the lowly likely price. The next is to focus on calming customer and receiving them used to banking on this new channel.

Automated Systems:

Automated systems have turned into very well-liked in the last a small number of existences. This is since they are usually fewer expensive than people who do the similar examine. For example, the charge of repairing an ATM is much lower than a person. Also, the machine can provide a 24 by 7 service that a person cannot do.

So, down with ATM's a diversity of other computerized systems has also been invested in bank branches. Other automated systems contain a cash machine, cash register or bank statements or debit card machines with pre-determined values.

Telephone Banking:

Telephone banking is the requirement of telephone bank services. Therefore, telephone banking is also prepared by as long as approximately all the services that can be obtained by a customary. Telephone banking, however, faces an extra face. Telephone bankers also want to indicate that they are talking to the right person or they may end up disclosing sensitive information to the wrong person. Ways have been developed to ensure this. Such methods include phone bank passwords and verification of individual in order that can only be provided by the account holder.

Phone banking gives customer extremely comfort as they can get service 24 * 7 anywhere. Also, telephone banking permits banks to lessen expenses as they are unable to contract out their call centers in low-cost countries such as India where work can be done at a lower cost and a win-win condition is created.

Internet:

Internet banking is provision of web banking services. Like telephone banking, online banking is used to repeat all resources provided by the branches. Also, like telephone banking, customer categorization is a trouble. Online banking face various risks such as cybercrime and cybercrime. However, technological advances have permissible banks to develop locked systems that can keep them from harm.

The major cause for the huge pressure on online banking is that the dispensation power is moved from bank employees to customer. So, if the customer wants a bank account, he gets himself. The need for bank employees is totally removed and this helps the bank to keep huge expenses. Some banks allege customer's exorbitant fees when they receive a service from a brick and mortar bank branch that can be found online.

Smartphone:

The banking business believes in mobile banking is the prospect of the business where public is gifted to access some service they need at the click of a few buttons. Technology therefore permits banks to provide customers with unprecedented levels of service while at the same time providing their shareholders with an unprecedented return on equity,

Consequently, the forerunners of the banking industry recognize that their business is already technologically advanced and the next industry leader will be someone technology to a high standard.

ONLINE ENQUIRY AND UPDATE FACILITY IN BANKING

In simple terms, a search management system is automated software that works on your front line so that all new queries are handled with proper care. Inquiries are entered, tracked, and managed systematically so that sales teams do something.

Bank customers, who currently have an Aadhaar card or their details are not updated or incorrect, can now head to the bank branch near the registration and update point. By providing Aadhaar registration and renewal space within the banking branches, customers can now find their Aadhaar problems easily resolved.

PIN

A personal identification number, or PIN, is a set of at least four characters used to open a bank account or credit card. PIN is required to contact the funds in the bank account with the bank card and to receive the advance payment by credit card.

Personal identification number (PIN) is a safety system to confirm the individuality. Alike to a code word, the PIN be supposed to be reserved private since it permits admission to vital services like monetary services. PINs can be used on anything digital and need right to use.

This could comprise communication devices, car locks, home locks, and much more. Common use of PINs at ATMs, online transactions, computer access or website access, etc.

If your debit number and PIN is known to someone else you can use it to purchase an item / bookmark Tkt etc even without a valid debit card. So make sure your PIN is not disclosed to anyone, including your close relationship. Because money is a poison that damages long-term relationships.

PIN SECURITY

PINs protect order and resources, therefore PIN that is hard to forecast.

Long PINs take lot of time to guess it. a lot of safety system close downward the account after a put number of attempt which ensure that it hard for thief and computer system to effectively supposition your PIN.

Because the PIN permits you to admission sensitive information, it is important to keep the number confidential.

Receiving and changing your bank PIN

If you do not know the PIN of your bank card, you may need to request it from your financial institution. In some cases, you cannot select your primary PIN; your service provider may send you a PIN separately from any card, in case your card is stolen at the post office.

You usually have the option of changing your PIN, and you may need to do so.1 However, some banks permit you to choose your own PIN as your card is printed.

If the PIN is lost or forget then reset which need to come for an electronic mail or document sent, visit your bank, or calling your security manager.

SIGNATURE STORAGE AND DISPLAY

Signature storage and retrieval system includes a system in which signatures are scanned and digitized, as well as associated digital code information, such as bank account numbers, which are stored in data processing sources.

A digital signature is something that banks can use to improve their portfolios. ... By making their services digital by signing up for banking. For example, if a bank uses a faster digital signature, it will be able to give more customers a limited amount of time.

Signature cards are those that banks use to identify the appropriate signatories for both personal and business bank accounts. ... These signatures serve as an additional confirmation tool for informants and customer service representatives that these signatures are used for comparison to permit checks and withdrawal slips.

All banks have signature recording software. This software records the signature of the customer at the time of the account opening. If the software finds any discrepancy it means that the bank is embarrassing your check. Industry experts say handwritten signature verification is done to verify the identity of the customer.

CHEQUE TRUNCATION SYSTEM

Truncation is the process of stopping the actual check issued by a cabinet from time to time as the bank introduces a route to the payment bank branch. . Reducing checks therefore avoids the need to deliver portable tools to all bank branches, except in exceptional cases for cleaning purposes.

The Check Truncation System (CTS) is the process in which checks are cleared electronically in its place of dispensation a bodily check by a bank which introduces a path to a paying bank branch. It is a pace engaged by the Reserve Bank of India (RBI) to subject a make sure right away.

The Check Truncation System (CTS) is a checking system developed by the Reserve Bank of India (RBI) for immediate checking. As the name suggests, termination is the process of stopping the flow of a visible check in its path of clearing. In its place the electronic image of the check is transfer with the most important data.

The Check Truncation System brings excellence to all processing and checking services and offers much profit to banks such as time and cost savings, cost effectiveness, including employee efficiency, restructuring business process and improved customer service.

The Reserve Bank of India (RBI) launches the pan-India CTS in September 2020 to make the removal of the check safer and faster. Recently, it was mandatory for all banks to implement the Check Truncation System (CTS) at all their branches nationwide in September.

CTS will be a great move to Digital India. IMPS, RTGS and NEFT have changed in the banking sector. Checks are still one of the leading payment methods in India, and a quick checkout cycle with CTS will definitely result in better customer information. It will also make the system more efficient, less expensive and safer for banks.

Benefits of Check Truncation System

- Time, money and staff spent on transferring checks from banks to payment room are eliminated
- Eliminate unreasonable related fraud
- Chances of misplaced checks during shipping are eliminated
- CTS are highly developed and highly secure.
- Provides quick approval checks

- Reduce operational risks and risks associated with paper handling
- There is no additional charge for collecting checks drawn on the inside grid bank, and does not provide area limits.

Highlights of Check Truncation System Checks

- All CTS checks hold a watermark, with 'CTS-INDIA', which is able to be seen when held in any light basis.
- Pantograph (wave-like design) with the hidden / embedded word 'VOID' obviously noticeable in the copies of the check

SECURITY MEASURES IN BANKS

Banks know that cyber security dangerous part of deliver greater customer examine. To keep away from becoming a statistic, understand your bank's cyber security points.

Locate facts of the economic group made banking online protected through analyzing its protection protocol and retreat regulations. For your personal security, financial institution on line with a monetary group of website online use a mixture of the commonplace bank safety features.

7 Bank Security Features That Protect Your Money

Encryption

Encryption hurts the information you edit online and reconfigures by use "keys" that make it clear. Seem for a web address that begin with "HTTPS" instead of "HTTP" - section of the web address indicate that all connections between your browser and website are encrypted.

Digital Certificates

The Secure Sockets Layer, often known as a digital certificate, verifies the website's legitimacy. Because it is utilised by third-party firms like Entrust and VeriSign, this development is known as "third-party authentication" or "third-party authentication." TD Bank, The bank name appears in the green bar that displays immediately before the web address in your browser's address bar on some banking websites, such as Bank of America's.

Verification

Verification examines ownership of the bank's website by the customer, swhich all party know that the additional is legal. The diversity of features to verify your password is used by Bank.

Biometric approval identifies persons with bodily attributes. Like of these technologies include fingerprints, voice stamps, scanning and facial gratitude. Their accurateness comes from that we are not in the exact same characteristics for two different people, which makes biometrics an effectual instrument for preventing deception.

TD Bank customer can sign up for TD Voiceprint. The banking software program catches the customer's voice at some point of the registration chat with the customer support diplomat. The voiceprint is saved firmly, and the customer can use it to bypass security queries while login.

Secure messages

Provide cozy methods to contact your financial institution and protect you from phishing scams and other scams. Fraudsters ship you e-mails along with your banks, seeking to entice you to reveal sensitive facts while replying to fake emails.

PNC Bank presents secure email similarly to a few other interactions on its customer service web page.

Limited Login Attempts

If wrong password is entered than a caution comes that additionally motive your account to be blocked. This is from bank's side of securing accounts. Limited login tries decreasing the possibility of hateful assaults by locking users out after a small variety of wrong password entries.

Farmer's investments Bank, as an example, permits 3 attempts. After that, customers reset their passwords by means of call customer service or assembly an online request and confirming us through e mail. Landmark National Bank additionally restricts users from trying 3 times earlier than remaining account getting right of entry to.

Fraud Alerts

Monitoring consumer debts with strange action indicators basis as a vital benefit defense instrument as it permits banks to fast seize fake and illegal use. Banks use fraudulent warnings to tell customer see debts may be compromised.

Conduct to keep individuality while Banking

In adding to the safety offerings offered by way of online banking establishments, defensive trial to defend yourself and your cash from deception.

1. No longer split your password or touchy private in order.
2. Make a complicated code word that is tough to gamble, or exchange it regularly.
3. Update the financial records frequently for check for unauthorized sports.
4. Update internet browser often to make certain your safety episodes updated
5. By no means use your email account to split account information - use your bank's safe messaging feature.
6. Get in touch with your bank right away if you see doubtful action in the account.

•

MODULE - 5
BANKING TECHNOLOGY

The technology and digitalization transform the BFSI sector by making it real-time data to make informed decisions, create competitive profits and enhance consumer knowledge. This also permits banks to share potential products, sell more, sell more, and strategically plan with customers.

In IB technology, banks advise software companies in the Internet, hardware / hardware, semiconductors, and IT services markets for integration, acquisition, and credit disbursement and equity.

The business intelligence system provide data on historical, current and prospect trend. This data help banks in a method that they can make knowledgeable decisions and therefore can bring about a total increase in output, efficiency and abundance.

The latest banking tackle offer features such as the aptitude to transfer funds among accounts, pay off loans, send personal payments, and check remotely using a Smartphone app. Automatic phone banking and online chat bots offer added comfort. Technology has made banking faster.

RTGS INFORMATION TECHNOLOGY

RTGS stands for Real Time Gross Settlement. Gross Settlement is a folder-moving mechanism in which money is sent in real time and without delay. Once the transfer process has begun, this electronic wallet technology allows the sender of the sender to have direct access to the payer / beneficiary. Gross Settlement refers to the distribution of entity activities rather than a sophisticated collecting system.

Money can be sent using RTGS (Real-Time Gross Settlement) through net banking. To begin such a process, gather certain information about the payer, such as account number, bank name, IFSC code, and account manager name. Another advantage of this phone transfer method is that the transaction can be listed ahead of time.

The RTGS payment system is maintained by the Reserve Bank of India (RBI) and is therefore a secure, consistent way to send and receive money at any instance in the state. In information, RTGS is one of the best ways to drive money to anybody. It is much quicker than the NEFT payment technique.

FEATURES

Here are the basic features of RTGS work that one should be aware of before using it:

1. Real-time online money transfers
2. Used for high value transactions
3. Safe and secure
4. Reliable and supported by RBI
5. Immediate removal
6. Individual contributions
7. Individual activities and on a complete basis

There are two ways to do RTGS:

a. Online banking:

Many banks offer an online banking platform using an online banking platform. After you have successfully added beneficiaries, you can transfer funds to the beneficiary. In addition to individuals, corporate account holders can also use online banking to make RTGS transfers.

b. Branch:

Visit your nearest bank branch and complete the RTGS form to start transferring funds.

BANK NET

Net Banking, also known as Internet banking or Internet Banking, is an electronic payment system. It permits you to do a lot of kinds of online transactions from the calm of your own home.

Online banking means logging into your bank account and performing online financial transactions on your Smartphone, tablet or computer. It's fast, usually free and permits you to perform tasks, such as paying bills and transfers, without having to stay or call your bank.

Internet banking, often known as net-banking or online banking, is an electronic payment system that allows customers of a bank or financial institution to conduct financial and non-financial transactions through the internet. Unique user / customer IDs and passwords protect online banking sites.

You can use Net Banking to make personal payments if: You have a payment address and bank account in India. Your purchase price is Indian Rupee (INR). Your bank is supported by a payment partner, Times of Money.

ADVANTAGES OF INTERNET BANKING

The advantages of internet banking are as follows:

Availability: You can use the banking contributions at any time throughout the year. The majority of the services are not time-limited; you can check your account balance at any time and change your price range without having to wait for the bank to open.

Simple to use: Online banking makes it simple to use the services available. Many people feel that transacting online is easier than going to a branch to do the same thing.

Convenience: You no longer have to leave your regular jobs in the rear of the car and wait in a bank branch line. You can carry out your transactions from any location. On-line banking can be used to pay application bills, regular deposit account installments, and other things.

Time Saving: With internet banking, you may complete any transaction in a matter of minutes. Funds can be sent to any account within the company, or a hard and fast account can be opened.

Activity Tracking: You might receive an acknowledgement receipt when you create a transaction at the financial institution department. You have the ability to reduce it. In conclusion, any transactions made through a financial institution's internet banking gateway may be verified. If necessary, you can use this as proof of the transaction. Details such as the payee's phone number, bank account number, and amount paid, as well as the date and time of the fee, and any remarks, if any, may be noted.

DISADVANTAGES OF INTERNET/ONLINE BANKING

The disadvantages of internet banking are as follows:

Internet Requirement: To use internet banking services, you must have a constant internet connection. If you don't have access to the internet, you won't be able to use any of the online services. Similarly, if the bank's systems are down due to a technical issue on their end, you won't be able to make net banking donations.

Security of Transactions: On-line banking transactions are still vulnerable to hackers, regardless of how many security precautions institutions take to ensure a secure population. Regardless of the advanced encryption measures used to keep consumer information secure, there have been instances where transaction data has been compromised. This may also constitute a significant risk, such as the hacker's illegal use of the records for personal gain.

Beginner's Difficulty: There are people in India who have made a living by living a long way from the internet. It's possible.

Password Protection: Every internet banking account requires you to enter a password to gain access to your donations. As a result, the password serves an important purpose in maintaining honesty. If the password is found by others, they will exploit the information to commit fraud. Furthermore, the chosen password must adhere to the requirements set forth by the banks.

Individuals should change their passwords on a frequent basis to avoid password thievery, which might be difficult to remember by the account user themselves.

SIGNIFICANT TASKS MADE EASY WITH INTERNET BANKING:

Online banking allows you to conduct a variety of financial and non-financial transactions. The following are some of the most popular items:

- Make a fund transfer
- Reviewing financial statements
- Making a fixed deposit (FD)
- Requesting a new chequebook
- Obtaining a new Debit Card PIN
- Applying for loans; paying taxes, utility bills, insurance premiums, and so on.

DATA NET

A facts network is a system designed to switch records from one network get admission to point to yet another or extra network access points through statistics switching, transmission strains, and gadget controls. Data networks and information networking answers impact almost all contemporary day communication, consisting of telecommunications and the Internet.

Generally, data networks are defined **by their ability to transmit signals via packet switching**. The data message is broken down into discrete bits called packets, and these packets are then sent over a digital network that uses an optimal route to minimize lag in data networking speed.

Data NET is a entire suite of software applications that permit give up-to-cease conversation between area employees and remote property and host workstations. Whether you're tracking and messaging personnel, far off cell assets which include motors, vessels or trains, or communicating with far flung pumps or weather stations, Data NET offers you with the platform that enables you to speak on a Global foundation.

FEATURES

- It can be established on any Windows based totally pc, permitting entire manager of the software without the value and lack of manipulate associated with an outside company
- Multiple terrestrial and satellite tv for pc network interfaces
- Built-in net, electronic mail and SMS servers
- Mapping assist which include ESRI,Google, Bing and OpenStreetMap
- Works with static and dynamic cellular addresses
- Can paintings as a non-public routing hub for optimum protection
- Works as a public nearby or national IP router
- Integrates with legacy structures and third-celebration applications
- Works with ODBC databases (SQL Server, MySQL, etc.)

VIRTUAL BANKS

EVOLUTION OF VIRTUAL BANKING IN INDIA

We live in a globalised world now. Traditional globalization is the initial option for international organisations all over the world. Technological advancements have made the world a much simpler place. There has been significant progress, especially in the areas of concern, storage space, gaining, and data transport. The planet has shrunk to the size of a "global valley."

Banks have home branches and provide online banking servic es. Banks have improved their worth sequence in a variety of areas, including computr programming, telecommunications, ATMs, and n ow EBanking.

The term "internet banking" refers to the use of the Internet to provide Banking services from a distance. It means that any user wi th a computer and a browser can access his or her bank's website an d verify any visible banking activity. Working on an online account can successfully reduce the number of bank visits. As a result, onlin e banking has reduced the number of interactions required to compl ete a task or solve a problem. Banks' traditional branches have evolv ed into PC networks, where customers may access all of a bank's rei mbursement and services with a single mouse click. There will be n o problems if bank branch offices are connected via ground or satell ite links.

At present, virtual banking means the provision of bank-related services by utilizing the most information technology without having to obtain direct banking assistance by the customer. These changes have a huge impact on the banking business..

The virtual bank can be described as a "non-branch bank", while the virtual bank is a provider of banking services through electronic devices such as ATMs, telephones, personal computers and / or the Internet. The purpose of this study is to investigate how different bank forms are taken or seen in India. The findings of this study may help both bankers to develop their own marketing strategies to promote tangible banking and researchers to excel in virtual banking studies and virtual reality organizations.

Some of the distinctive features of visible banking are:

- eliminate common location restrictions as it can arrive at customers in dissimilar countries / official area. This raises the question of how the law / regulatory system should be used by those businesses,
- The security of banking transactions, the validity of the electronic contract, the privacy of customers, etc., which has always been a problem for both banks and executives consider different factors when considering the Internet as a public domain, which cannot be controlled by any single authority or user group

Virtual banking is quite helpful in eliminating any human errors associated with paper management and improper data handling. This is automated, reducing the customer's reliance on live assistance. As a result, virtual banking enables banks to better serve their consumers by lowering service costs and increasing interest rates. Customers can summarise the benefits of visible banking in five words: comfort, space, speed of performance, efficiency, and efficiency. Because the internet is available 24 hours a day and can be accessed from anywhere in the world, virtual banking is incredibly convenient for users. In most situations, the process is as quick as pressing urgent buttons on a computer screen, and it is usually faster than using an ATM. Because banks can access and manage many accounts from a single online banking account, it works quite well. Customers who shop online can take advantage of a variety of benefits.

There are still some significant obstacles in the way of this type of service. One-on-one bank failure is a period of immobility and service disruption that can occur at any time, putting thousands of online bankers out of work and costing banks a significant amount of money to fix exchange errors and record data. Competitive advertising from competitors that are unconcerned about their customer is also common in Internet-based sectors.

SPECIALISED SERVICES IN VIRTUAL BANKING

In general, banks provide a variety of services to their customers, including: • An ATM is a machine that disburses cash and sometimes accepts deposits without the assistance of a human bank teller. Additional features are available at some ATMs.

• Mobile banking refers to the use of a mobile phone to conduct banking transactions. • Internet banking refers to the use of the Internet to conduct transactions, payments, and other activities.• IVRS Facility is also provided by banks that help in knowing account balances.

• Certain banks also provide services at door step.

• The customer can avail 24 hours banking facilities as per his convenience

Mobile banking (also known as M-banking or SMS banking) is a term for doing balance checks, account transactions, bills, credit applications, and other financial transactions using a mobile device such as a smartphone or a Personal Digital Assistant (PDA). SMS was used to deliver the first mobile banking services. In 1999, when the first basic smart phones with WAP capabilities were released, allowing users to access the mobile web, the first European banks began to offer mobile banking to their customers on this platform. Until recently (2010), the most common methods of mobile banking were SMS or the Mobile Web. Apple's early success with the iPhone, as well as the rapid growth of phones based entirely on Google's Android (operating system), has resulted in an increase in the use of distinct consumer packages, known as apps, that are downloaded to the mobile device.

According to the version of Mobile Banking, there are three types of mobile banking.

Mobile Accounting, Mobile Brokerage, and Mobile Financial Information Services are all examples of mobile financial information services. The majority of the courses in precise Accounting and Brokerage are transaction-based.

Customers who use online banking (or Internet banking) can conduct financial transactions on a secure website run by their retail or digital bank, credit union, or building society. Many functions and abilities are shared by all online banking solutions, however there are a handful that are often application particular. The not-so-unusual characteristics can be divided into numerous categories: Interactional (e.G., appearing a economic transaction consisting of an account to account transfer, paying a invoice, twine transfer, observe for a mortgage, new account, and so on.) • Third-party payments, as well as bill payments and telegraphic/wire transfers • Transfers of funds from a consumer's personal transactional account and their savings bills • Purchase or sale of an investment • Loan programmes and transactions, including repayments

THE COMMON FEATURES FALL BROADLY INTO SEVERAL CATEGORIES

Transactional (e.G., performing a monetary transaction including an account to account transfer, paying a bill, twine switch, observe for a mortgage, new account, and so forth.)

- Payments to 1/3 events, inclusive of bill bills and telegraphic/twine transfers • Funds transfers between a patron's personal transactional account and savings debts
- Investment buy or sale
- Loan applications and transactions, along with payments of enrollments Non-transactional (e.G., online statements, cheque e-book request)
- Viewing recent transactions
- Downloading bank statements, as an example in PDF layout
- Viewing pix of paid cheques
- Financial Institution Administration Features commonly unique to Internet banking consist of: Personal financial control support, which includes uploading data into non-public accounting software. Some on line banking systems assist account aggregation to permit the customers to reveal all of their debts in one region whether or not they're with their principal financial institution or with different institutions.

Telephone banking is a contributor provide by an economic organization, which lets in its customers to carry out transactions over the cell phone. Most phone banking offerings use a mechanized Smartphone reply system with phone keypad response or voice recognition capability. To guarantee safety, the patron have to first authenticate thru a numeric or verbal password or through security questions. With the plain omission of cash withdrawals and deposits, it gives certainly all the occupation of an automatic teller machine: account stability data and listing of most up-to-date transactions, electronic invoice payments, price collection transfers among a consumer's money owed, and so forth. Usually, customer also can talk to a live agent located in a call centre or a department, even though this option isn't continually assured to be offered 24/7. In addition to the self-service transactions listed earlier, telephone banking representatives are commonly skilled to do what changed into in the past to be had handiest at the department: mortgage programs, funding purchases and redemptions, cheque e-book orders, debit card replacements, exchange of cope with, and so forth.

The Interactive Speech Response System (IVRS) is a technology that allows a computer to communicate with humans by using voice. In telecommunications, IVR allows customers to interact with a company's database via a telephone keypad or speech recognition, after which they can answer their own questions by following the IVR instructions. IVR systems can answer with preset or dynamically created audio to guide users on how to proceed in the same way. IVR programmes can be used to control nearly any feature that can be broken down into a sequence of simple interactions. The IVR systems in place in the community are designed to handle large numbers of calls. For hands-free operation, the IVR era is also being incorporated into automobile systems. Satellite navigation, audio, and cellular phone systems are currently being used in automobiles. It has become commonplace in a variety of businesses

As a result, virtual banking is extremely beneficial in eliminating any human errors related with paper management and incorrect information deals. This automation also decreases the customer's reliance on live assistance from financial institution tellers for simple transactions and statement printing. In terms of cost, digital banking provides banks with new ways to keep funds and sell their goods more efficiently. Banks have the ability to reduce operating costs related with operational expenses such as building hire. As a result, digital banking enables banks can provide better deals to their customers by lowering service costs and raising hobby prices. As a result, the cost savings have a two-fold effect, benefiting both customers and banking institutions. Virtual banking, in general, refers to the provision of banking-related services through substantial use of information technology without the consumer having to go to the bank directly. Virtual

INTRODUCTION TO DATA MINING

We live in what is known as the "statistics age." We were collecting enormous amounts of data in this information age, since we believe that data leads to strength and achievement, and because of state-of-the-art technology such as computer systems, satellites, and so on. With the introduction of computers and the creation of a vast virtual garage, we began collecting and storing all kinds of data, relying on the power of computer systems to sort through this jumble of data. Those huge collections of documents, which were quickly saved on different systems, have unfortunately grown overpowering. As a result of the initial confusion, established databases and database management systems have emerged (DBMS). Effective database management structures were critical assets for managing a large corpus of data and, in particular, for effective and efficient retrieval of specific records from a large series at any time. The spread of information The expansion of database management systems has also led to the recent massive collection of various types of data. From commercial transactions and medical records to satellite images, textual content reviews, and naval intelligence, we now have far more records than we can handle. Information retrieval is clearly no longer sufficient for making decisions. When confronted with large amounts of data, we've developed new desires to aid us in making better managerial decisions.

These requirements include automatic statistics summarization, extraction of the "essence" of preserved statistics, and pattern discovery in raw data.

Data mining is a powerful new generation that has the potential to help companies focus on the most important information in their data warehouses.

It's been described as: "The automatic analysis of large or complicated records units if you want to discover good-sized patterns or tendencies that would otherwise go unnoticed."

The key elements that make statistics mining gear a wonderful shape of software are:

AUTOMATED ANALYSIS

Data mining automate the process of sift via ancient statistics with the intention to find out new information. This is one of the major variations among statistics mining and facts, where a version is typically devise by way of a statistician to address a specific evaluation trouble. It additionally distinguishes records mining from expert systems, wherein the version is constructed with the aid of a understanding engineer from regulations extract from the enjoy of an expert.

The stress on computerized discovery additionally separate facts mining from OLAP and simpler query and reporting tools, which can be used to verify hypotheses formulated via the person. Data mining does not rely upon a consumer to outline a particular query, simply to formulate a aim - along with the identity of fake claim.

Great or multifaceted facts units

Single of the attraction of records mining is that it makes it feasible to analyze very huge facts units in an inexpensive instance level. Data mining is also appropriate for multifaceted problems regarding comparatively little amount of facts however in which there are numerous field or variables to analyze. However, for small, relatively easy data evaluation troubles there can be easier, less expensive and extra powerful answers.

Data mining equipment can sweep thru databases and discover formerly hidden styles in a single step. The last significance of these styles will be assessed by a website professional - a advertising and marketing manager or community manager - so the effects ought to be offered in a way that human professionals can apprehend.

Data mining equipment also can automate the process of locating predictive information in big databases. Questions that traditionally required big hands-on evaluation can now be speaking back directly from the facts — quickly. A traditional example of a predictive problem is centered advertising. Data mining makes use of statistics on past promotional mailings to perceive the targets maximum in all likelihood to maximize go back on investment in destiny mailings. Other predictive issues encompass forecasting financial ruin and other forms of default, and figuring out segments of a population likely to respond in addition to given events.

TASKS OF DATA MINING

There are six basic types of data mining tasks:

Anomaly detection (outlier/change/deviation detection) - Identifying unusual data minutes that may be motivational or data errors that require further investigation.

Learning association rules (Dependency modelling) - Looks for relationships between variables. For example, data on customer purchase behaviours can be combined with supermarket strength. The store can utilise association rule learning to determine which goods are frequently purchased together and use this information for marketing purposes. Market basket analysis is a term used to describe this process.

Clustering is the task of discovering groups and structures in data that are "similar" in some way but not by any known structure in the data.

Classification is the process of generalising a known structure so that it may be applied to fresh data. An e-mail programme, for example, might attempt to classify an e-mail as "legitimate" or "spam."

Regression – look for a goal that resembles the original.

INTELLIGENT AGENTS

Intelligent agents include AI assistants such as Alexa and Siri, which employ sensors to detect a user's request and autonomously retrieve data from the internet without the user's assistance. They can be used to collect information about the environment it perceives, such as the weather and time.

An intelligent agent is a software programme that assists a user in completing a task or activity by automatically collecting information over the internet and communicating data with other agents based on the program's algorithm.

Businesses strive to increase revenue by attracting the ideal customers to their websites. Consumers are usually interested in comparing different products and services in order to find the greatest product at the best price. As a result, a wide range of intelligent agents working for buyers and sellers of products and services over the internet have emerged.

Importance of Intelligent agents

Intelligent agents are crucial in e-marketing and boosting an organization's eCommerce capabilities. It facilitates eCommerce transactions for both buyers and sellers by offering efficient, precise, and increased comprehensive web and information repository searches. Intelligent agents are highly interactive and capable of performing a range of activities in a variety of settings. Traditional search engines, spiders, and web crawlers are much less powerful and versatile.

INTELLIGENT AGENTS' CHARACTERISTICS

1. Mobility: Ecommerce intelligent agents move from computer to mputer, across various system architectures and platforms, gathering data until the search parameters are exhausted.
2. Goal-oriented: An intelligent agent can take a user's goal statement and carry out the task assigned to it. It has the ability to migrate from one location to another. machine to another and can act proactively in response to their

environment, and can exhibit goal-directed behavior by taking the initiative.

1. **Independent**: Intelligent agents function on its own without human intervention and must have the ability to make decisions .and to initiate action without direct human supervision. They communicate independently with repositories of information and other agents and accomplish the objectives and tasks on the behalf of the user.
2. **Intelligent**: Intelligent Agents are able to crawl for data more intelligently. They have intelligence to reason things out based on the existing knowledge of its user and environment and on past experiences. Intelligent agents follow preset rules **to evaluate conditions in the external environment.**
3. **Reduces network traffic:** Agents can swiftly communicate and collaborate with one another. This allows users to complete jobs quickly and efficiently, such as information searches, while also reducing network traffic.
4. **Multitasking:** An intelligent agent can handle numerous tasks at the same time. It frees the human user from repetitive clerical tasks.

Advantage of Intelligent Agents to Buyers

Intelligent agents can shop for a buyer, taking down parameters and returning with suggestions for goods that fit those requirements. Buyers can send intelligent agents to identify stores, brands, products, or service categories, as well as the required prices. Buyers can conduct comparisons even before visiting a seller's website thanks to these features. Intelligent agents reduce eCommerce expenses and increase transparency in online commerce.

Advantages of Intelligent Agents to Sellers

Sellers can use intelligent agents to act as "sales representatives" by offering product or service information and sales advice, as well as solving customer problems. Intelligent agents can be used by sellers to

a. track product demand,
b. track market share fluctuations,
c. engage in competitive knowledge mining, and
d. even gather knowledge through collaboration with buyer agents.

Agents assist businesses in gaining market knowledge and developing close relationships with their customers in an electronic world. Intelligent agents with more advanced capabilities can also negotiate with and learn from buyer agents.

BIOMETRICS

Biometrics is a method of verifying one's identity by measuring bodily attributes such as voice, fingerprints, face, retina, or iris of the eye, vein infrared thermogram, or a combination of these identifiers.

To determine likeness, biometric authentication compares data for a person's attributes to a biometric "template" for that person. First, the reference model is saved. To authenticate the data, it is compared to the person's biometric data.

There are numerous biometric IDs available:

- Finger/palm vein - this technique makes use of the unique vein patterns seen beneath the skin's surface in the fingers and palms.
- Fingerprint recognition – a method of authenticating identity by comparing two fingerprints. Mobile devices are particularly fond of this method[5].
- Voice/speaker recognition – recognising a person based on their voice characteristics (as opposed to speech recognition, which recognises what is being said).
- Face recognition — recognising a face using parameters such as relative location, shape or size of eyes, nose, jaws, and

more utilising various technologies such as computer algorithms or 3D sensors.

- Iris recognition - takes advantage of the unique patterns of each person's irises.
- Retinal scanning, also known as iris recognition, is the process of identifying blood veins in the human retina.
- Handwritten signature — a pattern of handwritten signatures can be used to identify a person.

Finding a biometric identification, on the other hand, is only the first step in making biometrics a viable banking technology. That's because any technique worth considering must meet the following criteria:

- be very secure,
- give protection against piracy,
- be socially acceptable
- be practical and easy to use, and
- be ubiquitous.

As a result, only a few biometric technologies have made it into the mainstream of banking. It's the finger vein, fingerprint, face, voice, and handwritten signature in particular. However, as some of the instances above illustrate, many financial institutions are willing to try even the most contentious technology if they feel they would improve security and customer experience.

Biometrics adding value to online banking

Banking has become increasingly digital in recent years, and biometrics can assist banks in providing better security and technology to customers undertaking online transactions. The biometric identification will never be forgotten or shared because it is based on identifying a person rather than a technology or piece of information. Furthermore, stealing biometric data is extremely difficult if the biometric vendor employs the proper architecture and security procedures.

As a result, biometrics alters the online payment system by relying on a customer's natural traits to validate their identification. It's similar to a personal password that can't be forgotten, lost, or stolen. Users don't have to remember the answers to security questions, and they don't have to carry a separate hardware token, therefore speed and performance are considerably enhanced. As a result, it is simple to use and contributes to the bank's customer trust.

How biometrics can be used to make a positive impact in banking

Keystroke biometrics

Keystroke biometrics, i.e. a personal typing pattern, can be incorporated to the online banking customer verification procedure in addition to fingerprints and facial recognition. Individual rhythm keystrokes, for example, result in a unique biometric template. This key click time can be recorded, saved, and compared in the future. Given the low cost of keystroke biometric verification, it can be simply deposited and utilised to verify online banking customers. This is a second-generation biometric authentication example.

Biometrics of the voice

There may be some persons who aren't educated enough to sign and do it themselves, or who don't fit the criteria for recognising financial institutions. In these situations, voice biometrics can help to streamline the verification process. Customers can utilise a voice or speech recognition technology to authenticate their identification in banking and customer service situations. Biometric technology is being used by banks to improve their sales performance and services in order to optimise commercial benefits. Biometric technology has helped to delight customer and deliver quality banking information through personal and needs-based engagement by providing simple and reliable verification.

Mobile Wireless Access Devices

The transmission of voice and data using radio waves is referred to as wireless. Employees can access corporate data without having to be physically connected to a network. Anything that sends or receives data over a wireless network is considered a wireless device. Mobile operators, as well as designated places, can connect to the wireless network.

From laptops to cell phones, a portable gadget is anything that can be utilised on the road. It is considered mobile as long as the place is not fixed. Despite their remote location, these are not considered cell phones. The transmission of voice and data using radio waves is referred to as wireless.

Mobile communication is the use of technology to communicate with persons in different areas without having to physically speak with them (cables or cables). A cell phone (also known as a mobile network, cell phone, or cell phone) is a wireless communication device. Cellular communication is exemplified by a cell phone (also known as a mobile network, cell phone, or cell phone) (wireless communication).

Wireless phones, like TV remote controls, radios, and GPS systems, are wireless gadgets. Phones, tablets, Bluetooth mice and keyboards, wireless routers, and a variety of other wireless gadgets are examples of other wireless devices. Another form of wireless device is a wireless charger.

CRM

Customer Relationship Management (CRM) is a term used in the banking industry, as well as other industries such as retail and commerce. Banks can use the Customer Relationship Management solution to better manage their customer and understand their demands so that they can deliver appropriate, faster answers.

Through its sales module, CRM supports banks in managing sales. It aids in the identification and conversion of references into potential customer. CRM aids in the discovery of new customer by utilising historical data and the amount of money they bring to the bank. CRM increases the efficiency of the marketing department's efforts.

As banking institutions became more competitive, customer relationship management (CRM) gained traction. CRM enabled banks to better understand their customers' present needs, what they've done in the past, and what they want to do in the future to achieve their objectives (Xu, et al., 2002). Despite the fact that many developing-country banks are as follows: India has understood the value of CRM and has put it into practise. Despite the fact that many developing-country banks are as follows: Although India has acknowledged the value of CRM and has deployed its operational systems, preliminary research suggests that CRM has actually harmed customer relationships. As a result, the purpose of this study is to use CRM to highlight the problems and challenges in India's banking sector. Furthermore, high-level meetings among various bank personnel have recognised some of the major difficulties in India's banking sector. Many authors have attempted to describe Customer Relationship Management in various ways. CRM is defined by Dyche (2002) in his book as:

Developing a comprehensive corporate grasp of customer preferences: Consistent customer information is the only way to build customer loyalty that encourages overall growth. This necessitates an awareness of each customer's wants and preferences. One of the most difficult difficulties facing banks is gaining a better understanding of their consumers and providing tailored service. It is obvious that Financial service firms will clearly no longer be able to achieve their growth and profit objectives using direct email campaigns that produce less than 1%. Those that do so will lose out to competitors who employ personal communication to direct the appropriate customer to the right product or service at the right time. To make the customer experience better

Improving distribution and channel management: How do store banks respond to intense market competition? In order to position themselves with the next level of sales and improved services, banks are focused on developing, deploying and integrating their channels quickly and effectively. Their goal is to meet three objectives: • Improved and consistent service based on a complete customer perspective • Increased revenue through the adoption of new products.

• Improved profits through lower product development and service costs Forward Banks will simultaneously improve customer service and profitability through the implementation of an integrated CRM strategy.

Deepening relationships with its customers means that banks must provide their products and services through appropriate delivery channels that attract their customers. Posting multiple channels and integrating them at the business level gives banks a consistent and complete customer perspective. To be successful, this must include all service channels í both physically and physically

Safeguarding customer information: Protecting customer information: In addition to these difficulties, customer privacy and information security are under attack more than ever. Compliance with customer information rules becomes increasingly difficult as rules grow at all levels of performance. In this context it is important for banks to ensure that their customer information is protected from both internal and external threats. By preventing security breaches and avoiding losses, banks can see the ROI in investing in security. This makes protecting customer data a requirement for successful competition in the financial services market. Banks should balance security costs against the need to share information and customer service, while at the same time finding ways to protect critical customer and financial data for the purposes of risk management planning.

Increased acquisition of new customers The CRM solution should help the targeted bank based on the "value" it has brought to the bank, now and for the life of the customer (and more through "next generation" marketing). Clearly, customer understanding and strategies are the biggest difference for a bank. CRM solutions (people, applications, systems and processes) must support these strategies in order to find the right products and services for the right customer

RISK MANAGEMENT

"The rational formulation and implementation of a plan to deal with prospective losses" is how bank risk management is defined. Risk management processes in the banking industry are primarily concerned with limiting the institution's exposure to loss or risk and safeguarding the value of its assets.

The process of recognising, evaluating, and controlling threats to an organization's finances and earnings is known as risk management. Financial uncertainty, legal debt, technological challenges, strategic management failures, dangers, and natural calamities are all potential sources of risk.

Risk management implies that fully funded financial institutions, such as banks, are limited in their ability to offer much-needed business funding; it also implies that financial systems require more than banks. It also gives banking systems and other sources of lending support more stability.

Risks of E-Banking

Operational Risk

The most prevalent sort of e-banking risk is operation risk, often known as transactional risk. • Incorrect transaction processing • Data integrity, data privacy, and confidentiality compromises • Unauthorized access to the bank's systems • Contract non-enforceability, etc.

Human factors, such as negligence (by customers or workers), employee fraud, hackers, and so on, are a possible cause of e-banking operational risk.

Threat to Security

When it comes to banking transactions, the security of the transaction is crucial. Customers all want their transactions to be kept private.

However, because all information is available online, there is always the risk that someone will access it and misuse it. Hacking threats and illegal access to the bank's systems add to the security risk of e-banking.

Risk to Your Reputation

The importance of a company's reputation cannot be overstated. When it comes to electronic banking, if a bank fails to provide, it is considered a failure.

Money Laundering Risk

All transactions through the e-banking channel are done remotely. Therefore, it is difficult for banks to use traditional methods to detect and prevent criminal activities.

While there are certain money laundering rules in place, for electronic payments, their feasibility is questionable. Therefore, banks carry the risk of money laundering.

Cross-border Risks

The core idea of electronic banking is to extend the geographical reach of both banks as well as customers. This means that the expansion can go beyond national borders. This leads to several cross-border risks:

- **Legal and Regulatory risks** – There is a possibility about uncertainties regarding the legal requirements in certain countries and jurisdiction ambiguities of different national authorities.
- **Operational risk** – If the bank uses a service provider located in a different country, then it is difficult to monitor it causing operational risk.
- **Credit risk** – Cross-border transactions can increase credit risk. This is because it is difficult to appraise an application for a loan from a customer in a different country.
- **Legal Danger**

- There is a legal danger if there is a breach of the laws, regulations, or authorised processes, or when the legal rights and obligations of any parties to the profession are not established.
- Because e-banking is a relatively new sector, there is a great deal of ambiguity and uncertainty about key norms and regulations. This increases the likelihood of running afoul of the law.

Strategic Risk

- This risk is linked to concerns such as: • Creating a business strategy
- Having the resources to support the business plan
- In the event of outsourced activities, the vendor's credibility
- Any change in the workplace can be stressful for employees.
- The level of technology used in relation to what is accessible, and so on.

Other Risks

Credit risk, liquidity risk, interest rate risk, market risk, and other hazards associated with electronic banking are similar to those associated with traditional banking. However, because of the usage of channels and the lack of geographical boundaries in e-banking, these risks increase.

All of the foregoing hazards could develop as a result of design flaws, insufficient technology, careless employees, or illegal system access (intentionally or not). As a result, banks must employ adequate technology and systems, as well as have proper access to a secure environment.

IMPACT OF TECHNOLOGY ON BANKS

In the banking industry, technology has opened up new goods and services, new markets, and efficient delivery routes. IT also gives the banking industry a framework to face the difficulties of today's competitive market. It is now easy to cut the cost of international transfers with the help of technology.

All areas of banking operations, including storage, processing, and data gathering, have been touched by technology. The following are some of the most damaged or affected places in banks:

Monitoring of the loan (Credit Schools)

A credit bureau was founded or aided by technological advancements. The system calculates customer pay records in order to give information that aids banks in pricing decisions and deciding who to borrow from. Software applications have been able to give banks with file entry, verification, and input tools thanks to advancements in technology. Data gathering enables banks to provide credit reporting services such as re-credit, customer credit operations monitoring, and fraud protection.

Debt management programmes and debt tracking services are available. Today's credit bureau infrastructure allows banks to gather, upload, verify, store, and communicate both positive and negative data, as well as supplementary information (e.g. court judgments, legal issues etc.). Information technology development and management Because the Credit Bureau has complete authority over all credit bureau processes affecting the banking industry. C++, C Sharp, Java, Oracle, and SQL are some of the programmes utilised in a credit bureau. All of these programmes contribute considerably to the credit bureau's overall success.

Economics and Competitiveness Banks have been forced to cut their interest rates or interest rates due to competition. Bank loans made recently Rather than seeking to become bigger banks, banks are attempting to attain a greater level of value in the banking system (acquiring more assets, taking higher risks etc). Due to the current economic climate, banks have tightened lending standards and credit regulations. Banks aim to safeguard their best and most innovative business structures in order to maintain a competitive economic scale.

Banks' Competitivity The rate of bankruptcy is being influenced by technology. The high level of expertise held by banks is eroding as a result of technological advancements. New competitors have developed, and many of the barriers that banks once provided have been lowered, and security breaches are now extremely close. Other financial services, goods, and services will become more visible. The participation of banks is increasing as a result of the decrease in inflow and construction of other banks.

The Economy of Service Delivery is Affected by Technology The way banks distribute financial goods to their consumers has been changed by technological advancements. Other kinds of service delivery, such as the Internet, electronic transfers, ATMs, and many more, have emerged as a result of technological advancements, reducing network dependency as a fundamental delivery mechanism. Currently, delivery systems offer a lot of financial systems through duplicate networks, which allow or encourage banks to change their delivery strategy, streamline their branch network plan, and provide or develop a number of delivery possibilities.

An online bank can be characterised as a financial institution that provides account balances and certain purchasing capabilities to consumers who sell on the Internet. Internet banking, often known as online banking, is a result of technological advancements. Technology's web development has resulted in a plethora of bank transactions and profession opportunities. Some of these pursuits are:

Positive impact of technology on banking sector:-

Digitization is the major uprising in banking.

- The banking procedure is faster and more dependable than before, and the preservation and recovery of documents and records has become considerably faster.
- Mechanized banking benefits the core banking system as well. All branches of the CBS (core banking system) have access to the same centralised data and are networked.
- The MICR cheque processing system has made the processing of checks much faster and more efficient than before.
- It provided better clarity in interactions.

- Technology also encourages competition among banks, resulting in greater services for customers.

Negative impact of technology on banking sector:-

- The main unenthusiastic crash of skill is job losses as automation has replaced the number of jobs in the banking sector.
- Technically comes the threat of Cyber Attack, loophole in the system, millions of data can be lost in an immediate.

●

MODULE-6
E-BANKING BUSINESS MODELS

INTRODUCTION

Today, current banking has a tendency to be active, adapt the commercial enterprise to the crucial adjustments that arise in worldwide markets and a brand new banking enterprise values targeted on end users. The commercial enterprise values of new banks with new commercial enterprise techniques, new managerial plan, and fresh commercial enterprise strategies based on net generation, distribution systems, pc and business intelligence can provide survival, increase, and improvement in each banking machine. The evolving development of information and conversation technologies transcends nearby time and limitations and greatly improves and helps the completion of monetary or banking transactions international. They have an impact on of the most powerful competition in the financial marketplace, in which the distance between banks, funding banks, coverage groups, purchaser housing is slowly declining, and so on. Financial enterprise plans are beneath regular strain to hold customers of its products and services, to reduce charges, to manipulate. Chance and use new technology and enterprise models.

The traditional banking fashions ruled the banking scene for extra than the 19th to overdue a long time of the twentieth century, while the form often furnished the content material place and wherein the financial institution cited the primary vicinity, without regard to needs and options Of its consumer, slowly but without a doubt dropping the war within the global monetary marketplace with current banking systems. current bank systems are based on its enterprise idea on new electronic banking strategies and fashions and offer a huge range of banking services and products, together with lively banking operations (acquisitions, belongings and legal troubles and adulthood), efficient banking operations (short-term and lengthy-time period operations) neutral banking business (banking activities and banking arbitrator commission

Banking services cope with the following banking functions - credit, savings, economic management, payment offerings, funding offerings, insurance, broking, banking financial institution, and actual property commercial enterprise. Banking structures that are seeking for to perform successfully and to insure against commercial enterprise risks need to adhere to the following banking business standards: economic coverage, professionalism and performance policy, safety policy, earnings management coverage, solvency policy and performance policy.

ELECTRONIC BANKING

Electronic banking (e-banking) is a modern-day enterprise representation that mixes the utilize of present day understanding, verbal exchange technology appearing banking sports at home, office, or on enterprise journeys, 24 hours an afternoon, 12 months a yr.

According to the Lexicon of banking, the digital bank offers a diversity of banking services. Depending at the technological competencies of digital data processing (banking pc use) or the banking offerings of bodily and criminal humans (agencies) furnished and made the usage of digital assist services.

Electronic banking is a form of banking enterprise and gives banking offerings to persons and corporate agencies, which can be supplied and operated through the usage of pc networks and social media (electronic help).

Electronic banking involves the performance of banking transactions the use of statistics and verbal exchange technology

Provides international connectivity, get right of entry to to banking services and facts, collaborative communique and different blessings to customer in the economic region.

- Completion of paper transactions and processing of guide transactions,

- Transfer bills all through fee (on-line), which appreciably will increase the rate of monetization,
- Operating expenses are stored low,
- Increase market share by means of introducing new sorts of business,
- Creating a brand new picture of the banking device that gives its customers with the ultra-modern generation solutions,
- Functional features of on-line verbal exchange,

The continuous improvement of electronic banking was motivated via many elements, which could be divided into 5 corporations:

- The improvement and use of modern-day facts and Internet-based totally communique technologies and Web technology relevant to economic offerings,
- Perform huge-scale virtual economic services (EDI Electronic Data Interchange) using a laptop network with extra services (VAN Value introduced resellers) that don't need to be part of the Internet and may not be support by using internet generation,
- Modern enterprise fashions based on new information and generation, which units the pc (digital) economy to be follow through monetary business plans;
- Reducing the regulation of banks and financial markets and the elevated competitiveness of economic business structures within the global economic marketplace,
- Implementation of ISO 17799 standards for security and facts safety in e-banking, ISO 7775 electronic messages for key files and the new ISO 15022 general, designed to lessen the time distribution of latest sorts of messages and advanced processing. Collateral,
- Modern economic security structures, such as passwords, protection agreements, smart playing cards, firewall, host server, cryptography, and biometric protection fashions

Electronic banking is an effort to combine various technologies (digital cash, ATM, POS / EFTPOS terminals, credit score cards, home banking, on line banking, net banking, cell banking, etc.), each emerged. In a extraordinary way. And in a extraordinary method, for the purpose of supplying a spread of banking services and products to cease users. Creating positive circumstances for the advancement of digital banking contribute to rising IT information for young humans, academic sports, decreasing the value of hardware and software program, and the price of banking offerings.

Under the have an impact on of technological alternate, it comes all the way down to the hard department of digital operations in banks:

1. The activities of centralized banks;
2. Electronic commerce with customers on their behalf:
    - Electronic banking trading,
    - Electronic banking of the business

MODELS OF ELECTRONIC BANKING

The growth of digital banking from the late 60 and near the beginning 70 of the 20 age and takes place in more than a few tiers

- **Proposal segment,**

  The make use of of records and telecommunication technology will become an expected element for hostile gain,

- **Stage of interactivity,**

  A sluggish change from the supply of banking offerings from offline to on line,

- **Phase of personalization,**

  Online banking services take the guide role in given that services to customers

- **Stage of virtualization,**

  A brand fresh fashion in banking is the appearance of digital banks (TeleBank-Virginia, Banknet-United Kingdom, and many others.) whose trade is base on providing on-line offerings that usually have decrease running and transaction prices.

Today, in contemporary bank structures survive in the following fashions and systems of digital banking:

HOME BANKING

Home Banking is used for domestic banking offerings without bodily presence inside the financial institution the use of a conversation hyperlink Domestic banking models from the United States in the mid-80s and their development became guided through the hyperlinks among the banking records gadget and bank customers, along with cellphone banking, online banking, on-line banking and mobile In the financial institution. The maximum widely used offerings at domestic banking stability and trading according to denarius, forex and financial savings money owed, records on unclaimed tests, loan statistics, transfers among money owed (RSD and FX), fee of monthly costs, catalog shopping, debt repayment. And loans, and so forth. Intended for a hit home banking, the consumer receives a PIN (personal identification wide variety - Personal Identity Number PIN) from a financial institution-enabled authentication server that handiest works for home banking customers which include application applications and databases for better records safety. In latest global, inside the advanced world, domestic banking is a fast-developing exercise that has an inclination to spread in less evolved nations.

HOME OFFICE BANKING

Is a version depending a home banking system in which personnel in a enterprise machine via their processor system (terminals) can utilize bank aid. Current banking structures for their customers give cash float organization classification and a entire collection of commercial enterprise plans (meting out all monetary dealings, on line monetary reporting, on line payment bills, finances making plans and monetary management, low-price hardware help, and many others.). Business plans that transfer the above functions to banks understand sure blessings in mind lessen office work, lessen the time required to method monetary transactions, store facts on a internet site, improve the service, and many others.

ONLINE BANKING

Is the paintings technique based totally on straight and stretchy message twenty four hours) among the bank and the customer processor device the usage of unique software (Microsoft Money, Manage Your Money, CornicheNet, and so forth.). monetary dealings (get admission to modern account balance and credit cards, late payments, transfers between bills, fixed and scheduled payments for automated transactions, time deposits, cash control offerings for what is needed to put in additional app software, and so on.) to be completed between the bank and the purchaser at the purchaser disk of the purchaser pc machine. Internet banking loses the importance of on line banking - steeply-priced software program and education time are required, restricting banking service users to concentrate on computer software that unique software should be hooked up and the extent of in order safety on the hard floppy is little.

INTERNET BANKING

Or Cyber banking has many direct users from quarters who bear out online economic transactions, because of the speed, performance, and efficiency of the transaction. Current banks with Internet Banking give their customers (persons and legal entity) worldwide 12 months-round (365 days) 2/7 offerings and monetary dealings. In order offerings encompass balancing and transaction in line with dinar, foreign exchange and savings debts, unregulated check facts, loan statistics, loan facts, and credit score card transaction facts, and card usage expenses, authorized records. Limit and credit score card transactions, transaction facts, collateral information, forex facts, and monetary transactions. Financial transactions include transfers among neighborhood forex financial institution debts, transfers among accounts without foreign exchange, cash purchase and sale of coins / overseas for ex, electronic charge of pre-ordered orders, loan payments, credit score payments with a credit card, card lock. If misplaced or lost. Banks in market do not get sum to make digital connections so one can pay in dinars and to shop for cash or small amounts.

Mobile Banking

A brand name new style in electronic banking wherein patron makes use of present day mobile phones (J2ME mobile phones, Blackberry, Windows Mobile, Android, iPhone and iPad), individual virtual assistants (PDAs), and personal computer systems palmtop ,portable computer packages over the Internet and WAP requirements whenever and anywhere in a relaxed and fast manner to carry out the subsequent banking transactions - take a look at account rates on all accounts and credit score playing cards, pay due payments, switch budget from account to account, carry out transactional transactions, take a look at expiration date inside the modern-day account, update unused checks, order tests, controlled forex account card, test alternate list, and so on.

With the enlargement of cell telephones. Mobile telephones will be bought global, so that it will increase by using 10.4% compared to 2010.) The boom of commercial enterprise using smart phones will increase. The telephone uses the standard for growing wi-fi programs for networks - WAP (Wireless Application / Access Protocol), universal organization portable connections - GSM (Global System for Mobile communications) and etiquette for wi-fi records transfer through GPRS (General Packet Radio Service). Smart phones (iPhone, iPod contact, Android, and so on.) and their apps, fitted cellular browsers and photo solutions offer a simple, smooth and relaxed (128-bit encryption) using cell banking services. The benefits of cell banking are pondered in mobility, relieve, accessibility, safety and economy money ,time.

PHONE CALL

A provider that permits customer to quick, without problems and effortlessly carry out cellphone banking offerings.

Telephone banking is supported - facilities wherein the "name center" is established The Web device permits the person to perform all the duties assigned to the customer the use of the user interface. - Automatic speech reputation (IVR) structures in which the consumer can take a look at account balances, transfer cash to other or authorized financial institution debts, meet credit card debt and deposit transactions. The requirement to apply IVR phone is able to dial tone.

SMS BANK

A banking provider in which a bank offers correct and reliable statistics to customers about the fame and modifications in their cell debts. SMS banking permits customer to apprehend the present day account balance after each change, to apprehend the modern account popularity at any instance request by using the purchaser, dealings via SMS ISP offerings, loan development facts and receiving bank advertising mail.

MODELS OF ELECTRONIC PAYMENT

When you buy items and services online, you pay for them the usage of an digital medium. This price approach, in addition to using cash or take a look at, is known as an e-commerce payment system and is also called on line or electronic price systems.

The growing use of on-line-based totally banking and purchasing has visible the increase of numerous e-trade price structures and technologies improved to decorate, beautify and offer comfy e-payment transactions.

Paperless e-commerce bills have modified the price system by lowering office work, transaction charges, and group of workers expenses. Systems that are simpler to apply and less time eating than in individual and assist groups growth their market access.

THE FAILURE TYPES OF E-COMMERCE PAYMENT APPLY TODAY ARE:

CREDIT CARD / DEBIT CARD

The most famous payment approach for e-commerce offerings is credit score cards. Easy to apply; the consumer must certainly input his or her credit card range and expiration date in the perfect area on the service provider's net page. To improve the safety gadget, extra security features, such as the usage of a card verification code (CVN), had been brought to on line credit card bills. The CVN device enables discover fraud by means of evaluating the CVN quantity with the cardholder records

Debit playing cards are the second one largest price technique for e-commerce in India. Customers who need to apply the Internet inside their economic limits favor to pay with their Debit playing cards. by a debit card, the purchaser be able to handiest reimburse for purchased items by the cash already in his or her bank account in place of a credit card in which the patron fees are charged and bills are made in. Quit of charge length.

Credit card fee is single of the majority lengthily used and popular techniques now not best in India but also on the global level.

As a worldwide charge answer, through permitting charge popularity by way of credit card merchants can reach the global marketplace.

Credit playing cards are easy to apply and relaxed. The purchaser ought to include the cardboard variety, expiration date, and CVV, provided as a precautionary measure. CVV permits detect fraud via evaluating consumer info with a CVV number.

When it comes to debit cards, it may be considered the following maximum famous shape of ecommerce payments.

Debit cards are generally favored with the aid of customer who store on-line within their monetary limits. The essential distinction among a credit card and a credit score card can simplest be paid with cash already inside the bank account, while inside the case of a credit card, the quantity used is charged, and bills are made ultimate of fee duration.

SMART CARD

It is a artificial card fixed in a microprocessor has the patron's personal records saved and can be loaded with money for on-line transactions and on the spot payment. The amount charged to the smart card decreases because the patron uses and must be re-deposited into his or her bank account.

The clever card is ready the size of a credit score card, fabricated from plastic with a microprocessor chip embedded that holds critical economic and private information. The microprocessor chip is loaded with applicable records and recharged periodically. In addition to those pieces of information, cash storage structures have been constructed at the chip. Card cash is kept confidential and secured to ensure the safety of the smart card solution. To pay with a clever card it's far critical to offer the card to the hardware terminal. The tool requires a special key from the issuing financial institution to initiate the switch of budget in any manner. Smart playing cards can be discarded or recharged.

A famous example of a discarded clever card is the one issued by way of telephone agencies. After the usage of the aforementioned quantity, the cardboard can be discarded. Smart playing cards were used significantly inside the telecommunications enterprise for years. Smart card era can be used to store fitness care facts, transportation, identification, trading, loyalty applications and banking, to call some. Smart playing cards enable facts for distinctive functions to be stored in a single region. A microprocessor chip can manner one-of-a-kind varieties of records, therefore, different industries use them in distinctive methods. Due to their multi-motive activities, their recognition in Turkey is likewise developing

Smart playing cards are broadly divided into groups: Contact: This kind of smart card have to be covered in a unique card observe to be examine and advanced. The clever communication card contains a microprocessor chip that makes contact with electric connectors for statistics transmission. Touch: This sort of smart card can be read remotely the usage of a radio frequency. The clever touch card additionally consists of a microprocessor chip and a word that permits records to be transferred to a special card reader without physical contact. This sort of clever card is useful for people traveling by means of car or on foot. They are extensively used in European nations to accumulate tolls, educate fares, parking, bus fare, and entry charges for movies, theaters, theaters, and so forth. Smart Cards can accommodate a ramification of applications that permit a customer to make purchases with a credit score card, financial institution account, or card financial savings. These cards could have more than one applications strolling simultaneously. The customer, as an example, may additionally have a widespread flight system that works on the identical card as the customer or credit score account. This permits the patron to earn factors in his or her favored program. Several laptop producers (e.G. Clever card may be programmed for one of a kind applications. Some cards include edits and statistics to support multiple packages, and a few may be updated with new programs after launch. IBM, Microsoft, Schlumberger, and Bull are among the major players within the improvement and use of smart playing cards.

Some of the blessings of smart card playing cards include the subsequent: • Storage of multiple forms of statistics • Not without difficulty duplicated • Not luxurious via their design and use. On the alternative hand, smart card applications are anticipated to increase because of the decision of these adverse conditions inside the near destiny.

E-Wallet

E-Wallet is a prepaid version that lets in the consumer to save most credit cards, debit card and financial institution account numbers in a comfy area. This removes the need for you to input your account records every time you are making a payment. Once a customer has registered and created an E-Wallet profile, they could pay right now.

E-pockets are certainly one of the approaching styles that offer absolutely new purchasing knowledge. The employ of e-wallets is suitable more and more well-known.

E-Wallets require registration from providers and customerele. Following growing an e-wallet account and connecting it to a bank account they can take out or put cash.

The entire system with e-wallet is simple and rapid. Measured a complex and fast digital price technique, e-wallets can be included with mobile wallets using higher features such as NFC.

Prepaid e-wallet accounts shop patron records and manifold credit score / debit playing cards and financial institution money owed. It requires most effective one registration and eliminates the need to re-enter facts on every occasion you pay.

The most useful electronic wallets for online stores are commercially available in packets, palm-sized, hand held, and laptop PCs. They offer a comfy, green, and transportable on line shopping device. They shop private and monetary records inclusive of credit score playing cards, passwords, PINs, and much more. To simplify the credit score card system, many companies are presenting electronic pockets services. E-wallets assist you to song your billing and delivery statistics in order that it can be entered with a unmarried click on taking part retailer web sites. E-wallets also can store e-assessments, e-coins and credit score card facts on multiple cards. A famous instance of an e-wallet available on the market is Microsoft Wallet. To get right of entry to Microsoft Wallet, one wishes to set up Microsoft Passport. After launching Passport, Microsoft e-wallet may be installation. After that, e-wallets may be used for small bills. They also remove the re-entry of personal facts into paperwork, ensuing in greater velocity and performance for on line consumers. Microsoft Passport consists of some of offerings that include the subsequent one-way login, pockets and infant passport services. A unmarried login carrier permits a consumer to apply a single name and password for a growing wide variety of participating e-commerce websites. The consumer can use on the spot purchases on-line with a pockets provider. The infant passport carrier permits protect and control the online privacy of kids.

NET BANKING

This is some other popular way to make e-trade bills. It is an clean way to pay for on-line purchases directly from the customer financial institution. It makes use of the equal technique as the prepaid debit financial institution card. Net Banking does no longer require the customer to have a card for allege purpose but the consumer needs to record with his or her financial institution to achieve a banking facility. When you entire the purchase the purchaser just desires to enter the financial institution identity and PIN.

MOBILE PAYMENT

One of the cutting-edge approaches to make on-line payments is by means of cellular cell phone. Instead of the usage of a credit attain or money, all a customer has to do is make a payment demand their carrier issuer via textual content message; a purchaser cell account or credit card is charged for the acquisition. To set up a cellular fee machine, the patron should down load the software program from its carrier issuer website and hyperlink a credit card or cell price facts to the software.

Payment receipt turned into distinct for mobile login.

This virtual price solution affords a brief solution for customer. To installation a cell fee approach, the customer needs to download the software and join it to the credit score card.

As ecommerce will become cell, customers discover it a lot less complicated to use mobile charge alternatives.

AMAZON PAY

Another easy, secure and short way to pay for on line purchases with Amazon Pay. Use the information saved in your

Amazon account to access and pay for the fine service provider web sites and apps. Your billing statistics is securely stored with Amazon and is on the market to lots of websites and apps you want to keep on.

If you plan to sell your products online, Amazon may be glad to help you in putting in place fee gateways to your products and services. You can also think about promoting on Amazon, one of the world's maximum popular e-commerce systems. To promote on Amazon, you can sign up for online income at no cost.

•